NASCAR IN PHOTOGRAPHS

Featuring contributions from **JUNIOR JOHNSON, RICHARD PETTY, CALE YARBOROUGH, BILL ELLIOTT** and **JEFF GORDON**

JONATHAN INGRAM

THIS IS A CARLTON BOOK

This edition first published in 2002

10 9 8 7 6 5 4 3 2 1

Text and photographs © Carlton Books

A CIP catalogue reference for this book is available from the British Library.

ISBN 1 84222 634 7

Printed in Dubai

Project Editor: Luke Friend
Project Art Direction: Darren Jordan
Production: Lisa French
Picture Editor: Debora Fioravanti
Design: Design Revolution

NASCAR IN PHOTOGRAPHS

JONATHAN INGRAM

CARLTON
BOOKS

Contents

Introduction

NASCAR founder "Big Bill" France was fond of saying the sands of time stand still for no man. An excellent mechanic and race car driver before he launched America's most successful sanctioning body in 1948, France's imagination was fuelled by the desire to get ahead of those sands and ride the future's ragged edge. His son and successor, Bill France Jr., often summed up his father by saying he was pretty good at seeing around the bend.

Big Bill, who once rode an elephant into town to promote a race, thought big, too. It was not by accident the sanctioning body he formed with help from other members of the racing fraternity in Daytona Beach eventually became such a big success. Or that his Daytona International Speedway became America's consecrated ground for stock car speed.

France didn't invent stock car racing, or even create the name NASCAR, which was coined by Red Vogt, the first in a line of brilliant mechanics who worked on the cars known as "stock" because they were initially replicas of those found on the showroom floor. A visionary businessman who knew there was plenty of money to be made after a decade of experience promoting races on the sands of Daytona Beach, France sought to better harness the passionate desire to build and race fast cars.

His first attempt in 1947 collapsed when France simply declared Fonty Flock to be the national champion after a handful of races dominated by the 1939 and 1940 Fords left over from the pre-war years and modified into full-time race cars. Even the presentation of a big trophy amidst a bevy of showgirls in swim suits at his Ebony Lounge on top of the Streamline Hotel in Daytona Beach failed to convince anybody that France was running something other than a minor regional circuit.

Then France rolled up his lengthy sleeves. He listened to some advice from journalists, among others, and held a series of meetings at the Ebony Lounge in December of 1947 with like-thinking racers who had already seen his ability to promote—and sometimes win—events on the beach. Out of those meetings, France created a sanctioning body known as the National Association for Stock Car Automobile Racing that promised to keep a regular schedule at tracks all over the country and crown a national champion. Thereafter, Big Bill alternately cajoled and hammered would-be participants, including the automotive factories, into a cohesive group that promoters and fans could count on seeing regularly, just like the Indy car drivers whose races had been sanctioned by the American Automobile Association on the Championship Trail since 1909.

Above: Lloyd Seay was among the first in a long line of men revered for their ability to pilot a roaring stock car. He was not the last to get his training as a whiskey driver.

Born in Washington, D.C., France's first raced during the Roaring Twenties on a board track in nearby Laurel, Md. aboard a Model T Ford surreptitiously borrowed from his father. He later made Florida his home to further pursue racing ambitions on the stretch of sand already famous for land speed record runs by the likes of Sir Malcolm Campbell in the Bluebird and the ingenious and nervy Frank Lockhart.

Lockhart, who began his career racing Ford Model T's on the Ascot track in Los Angeles as a teenager, won the Indy 500 in 1925 in his first attempt. Three years later he nearly died in the green-gray waves when his self-designed Stutz Black Hawk flew out of control during a record attempt on the beach. Lockhart returned to try once more in 1928 and met his doom when the Black Hawk barrel-rolled and crashed again. Within a few years those men who survived and their ilk soon disappeared into the wide-open tableau and hazy heat of the Bonneville Salt Flats.

In their place came a new breed of adventurers dancing on the edge of the tide. There was always more than a whiff of corn liquor—as well as the myth—around stock car racing. Among the participants were bootleggers, car owners and drivers alike, who made their living hauling moonshine out of the Appalachian Mountains down to the cities in Maryland, the Valley of Virginia, the Carolina Piedmont, north Georgia and Alabama. Not all were engaged in the untaxed liquor trade, but the presence of the moonshiners in the stock car races of the South raised the level of competition for everybody.

The same was true when the good ol' boys barnstormed across the Mason-Dixon line to such famed venues as the circular mile in Langhorne, Pennsylvania, where the Southerners intimidated the competition before the green flag ever fell.

"Several professional race drivers used to enter the big races," said the *Stock Car Racing Record* guidebook published in Baltimore in 1941, "but there were several

The early stock car events were not confined to the South any more than the modern version, because of the sport's appeal to the working class all over America. But its allure was greatest undoubtedly in the South, where honor, passion and bravery in the face of violent circumstances remained in high demand long after the humiliating defeat in what Southerners liked to refer to as the "War Between the States". A fast car had an intoxicating allure not only on the track, but in the rural backwoods, where it provided mobility without any loss of loyalty to the land, and provided a means to haul tax-free whiskey.

Above: *Cocky and easy going, "Big Bill" France could wheel a car or wield the power necessary to build NASCAR into a major sports and business attraction.*

good reasons from Dixie why the pros went to the movies instead of Langhorne this year."

France was one of the hotshoe barnstormers who won on the beach as well as in places like Ft. Wayne, Ind. while driving Fords owned by retired bootlegger Raymond Parks. Big Bill had developed a soft drawl in his deep, avuncular voice and was himself a forerunner of the good ol' NASCAR stars with syrupy tongues and lead in their toes. With a few rare exceptions, such as Fred Lorenzen and his latter day Golden Boy equivalent Jeff Gordon, NASCAR's biggest driving heroes all came from the South, as did most of the participants.

Although it wasn't played up that way in the newspapers, France was part of a triumvirate who drove in the early 1940s for the soft-spoken Parks, who quietly switched his business after Prohibition from moonshine to selling cigarettes in vending machines around Atlanta, a good and profitable cover for running

illegal slot machines in private clubs. Parks campaigned his fleet of three 1939 Fords prepared by Vogt in races for regular drivers and fellow Dawson County natives Lloyd Seay (pronounced See) and Roy Hall, and occasional sit-in France, who drove the spare entry when available.

Parks' cars were prepared specifically for the track, but the 1939 and 1940 Fords were ideal for both racing and bootlegging. Ironically, when loaded with a maximum capacity of 1,600 pounds of moonshine, the '39 and '40 Fords weighed the equivalent of a modern tube-frame stock car, roughly 3,500 pounds. But when pared down for racing, the Fords with their flathead V-8 engines, heavy-duty transverse leaf springs and evenly distributed weight were hell on wheels—especially if you were used to driving them flat-out with so much precious cargo in the dead of night.

As skilled and commanding as he may have been,

France was not stock car racing's earliest star compared to the phenomenal Seay. Known for his occasional two-wheel cornering technique used on the packed sands of the original Daytona Road and Beach Course's north turn, the legendary Seay unfortunately didn't live long enough to run a NASCAR-sanctioned event. His grains of time ran out only hours after he won Atlanta's Labor Day stock car race at Lakewood Speedway in 1941, driving car number 13 to his sixth major victory of the year. Seay was shot through the heart at age 21 that same night in a fight with a cousin over who would pay for a load of sugar, a key ingredient in moonshine.

A six-foot tall headstone—just about the height of the slender, sandy-haired driver—stands testament over Seay's final resting place in a little cemetery in Dawsonville, Georgia, alongside the standard markers for his father and two brothers in a small town graveyard full of sorrow, grief and belief, etched in messages about the hope of heaven and meeting again in the hereafter.

The large tablet-like edifice for Lloyd Seay has its own unique imprimatur. The stone may have the discolored tears of time dripping across its horizon, but emerging unblemished in 3-D relief from the concave surface are the smooth-as-sand, immortal carvings of the winner's trophy from Lakewood and a modified '39 Ford with a photograph of Seay himself appearing in the driver's side window, smiling cockily to the last.

This eerie grave is testament to the rough-and-tumble beginnings of the men who would be stock car racing kings. Stand beside Seay's red clay tomb and you can still hear the low rumble of a flathead Ford V-8 just over the pine-studded hills of Dawson County, hauling 1,600 pounds of half-gallon jars to beat the Depression, poverty, the Revenuers and anything else that might threaten a mountain man's independent way of life, liberty and the pursuit of speed.

Since then, we have seen Fireball, Curtis and The Last American Hero, sung the psalms of King Richard, lauded the Silver Fox, hailed Cale, Bobby, Jaws, Awesome Bill and Dale. Which one's the best or had the biggest impact? That depends on whether you're talking about the greatest in words as well as deeds, or races won, speeds attained, titles accumulated or

maybe whether a man's style behind the wheel liberated the spirit with that sudden warmth known by those who toss back white whiskey or by teetotalers calling up Jesus in a Revival tent on a sweltering summer's eve.

It's a bit like asking which events had the most impact upon the growth of the mechanized sport of kings. Was it France's first "Strictly Stock" race in Charlotte in 1949? Did the first high-banked superspeedway rising out of the sandy soil of South Carolina's up country near the sleepy town of Darlington change the NASCAR universe so indelibly it made Harold Brasington the sport's highest priest? Was the last lap of the first Daytona 500 in 1959 bigger than the last lap 20 years later when Donnie and Cale crashed cars and then fists into one another on the grass at Turn 3 as King Richard returned to his throne before a live television audience stuck indoors by a huge snowstorm?

Just over four decades after the hearse had left him at his final resting place, Seay paid silent tribute to another passing parade when the town of Dawsonville threw a party for a gangly kid named Elliott, yet another native son who had just won his first NASCAR Winston Cup race and would soon launch the awesome legend of "Million Dollar Bill". The tall, lanky driver and his two sandy-haired brothers all had come of age in the Winston Cup on the Ford team of their father George. Were all four the ghosts of the family Seay, rising out of the mist of time like white-skinned sycamores in a stand of green pines, roaring down from the hills of Dawson County once again, liberating themselves and the world?

George Elliott smiled that day of the parade held for his youngest son back in 1983 and then recalled from his Bible Belt education that a prophet is never honored in his own land. Maybe so. But the rules seem to work differently if, like Seay or that flashy kid named Gordon five decades later, you can ride the crest of time and bring home the field in a roaring stock car with nostrils flared and a big number blaring on a couple tons of sheet metal, iron and steel. Or if, like the steely-willed Big Bill, you can see far enough around the bend to create a racing series that constantly evokes heavenly myths as well as man.

Junior Johnson

One of the few men who participated in all of NASCAR's first five decades, Robert Glenn "Junior" Johnson became a legendary driver before moving to great success as a car owner. Johnson won 50 races, but then abruptly retired, leaving behind the reputation as a fiercely fast and uncompromising driver. As a car owner, he went on to win 139 races, six championships and $22 million in prize money. The former bootlegger helped to bring stock car racing its first national acclaim in 1965 when Tom Wolfe wrote the story of his transition from moonshiner to racer entitled, "The Last American Hero—Junior Johnson—Yes!"

You're best known for fast driving on the highways, but weren't you plowing behind a mule when you got a chance to drive your first Grand National race?

I was about 16 years old and they was having a little race there at North Wilkesboro. My brother had a pretty fast whiskey car, and he wanted me to come to North Wilkesboro Speedway and drive it. So I was in the field plowing, barefooted, overalls, no shirt on. And he drives up down close to the field and says, 'I want you to go to North Wilkesboro and drive my car in the race.' I said, 'Well, let me get my shirt and my shoes and I'll be ready.' And so that's how I wound up driving in my first race.

You've said that if you had not rolled a tractor over at the age of 14 and broken your arm, you would have ended up as a Major League baseball pitcher.

That's what I would have done if I hadn't have broke my arm, I think anyway. I think racing is great, but every kid has growing up a thing he'd like to be. And when I was growing up I'd like to have been a baseball pitcher. I was a great fan of the New York Yankees, Joe DiMaggio and all them guys. As an idol of them I devoted a lot of my youngster ages up 'til I broke my arm to baseball.

You also grew up in North Carolina's moonshining days, since your father was involved in the bootlegging business. What was that like?

When you grew up in the whiskey business like I did, you have almost as much excitement out of that as you do racing, because it's a race to win or you go to prison, you know. And that gets more exciting than beating some other race driver.

How did you feel about those terms?

I wasn't comfortable with it. To us, where we grew up, moonshining weren't really a bad thing. We didn't intend to hurt anybody. The only problem we had with it, the government, was that they wanted their tax money from it. And the whiskey runners just didn't pay the taxes on it. And that was really what was against the law that put them all in jail.

The Revenuers never caught you on the road, but did succeed in catching you at the still. What was it like for you to spend time in prison?

It's a miserable experience. I tell you I wouldn't take anything for the time I pulled, but I wouldn't want to pull any more. I went to prison and I knew I was guilty and caught, and did my time. While I was there I

Above: *Johnson showed no mercy for either his equipment or his adversaries. He could be expected to take the lead, crash while trying or break the car. In 313 starts he earned 47 poles and won 50 times, but failed to finish 165 of his races.*

Above: *In this wild ride, Johnson barrel-rolled his Pontiac down the beach in 1956—and then clambered out the back window. Such incidents only enhanced his reputation for fearlessness.*

learned a lot of things about ongoing life, such as you're not your own boss. Sometimes you think you are, but you're not. Somebody else can tell you what to do and you will mind and do what you're supposed to, and you can make the best of a bad situation if you try.

Was running whiskey different from driving a race car?
I don't think I ever had a race car that run any faster than what I had on the highway. Basically, training came from on the highway. About all the good drivers back in the early fifties on up to the mid-fifties in towards the sixties, take Bob Flock, Tim Flock, Curtis Turner, Gober Sosebee. All of them guys sometime or another had to haul moonshine.

What were the cars like that you drove while hauling moonshine?
You know, I had the fastest cars they had. Because you know when NASCAR was running pretty much that factory-made stuff, we was modified on the highway.

We was big motors, three and four carburetors, sometimes five, six, whatever it took to make a fast run, superchargers and turbochargers back in the forties. I've had cars that run so fast on a straight road that it looked like it was two foot wide, on down the road, you know. And I never had nothing like that on the racetrack.

What was the fastest you've ever driven on the track?
Probably the fastest I ran anywhere was in Daytona. I think about the time I quit we was running 180, 182, 183 miles an hour. But we brought a car to Daytona in 1951 and run on the beach out here, clocked 189 or something. It was a '51 Ford. Had a Cadillac motor in it, souped up, bootlegging car with a lot of horsepower. It had two four-barrel carburetors. You didn't have to go very fast often because most of the time we traveled late at night and the highway patrol you'd run up on every once in a while. But then you didn't have to run very fast for very long, because they didn't have nothing to compete with you.

Junior Johnson

Above: *Famed for his technique as a jackman, slinging the long-handled jack in a wide arc as he circled the car, Johnson filled in as gasman for his pit crews on occasion, too.*

What about the time the Revenuers hired Curtis Turner to try and catch you?

Well, they caught a moonshiner's car up in Virginia and they brought Curtis Turner down. They was having quite a contest of trying to catch me at that particular time. They paid him and brought him down to run me down. Of course, the car he had wouldn't do it.

All your NASCAR victories came on oval tracks, but you did sit on the pole the one time you ran the road course at Riverside.

That was right up my alley. Ford kept trying to get me to go to Riverside and run, because, you know, I was familiar with roads. And I wouldn't go because it exposed the driver to the wall. I think it's still foolish for a driver to go around a turn and him be the closest thing to the wall. That's suicide as far as I'm concerned. Parnelli Jones and Dan Gurney, all of them

Above: *A deadpan expression belied Johnson's ingenuity while beating the opposition and NASCAR's rulebook.*

boys had run out there for years, and I never been there before and sat on the pole.

You're credited with inventing the bootlegger's turn, a 180-degree swap of either end of the car on a two-lane road while at speed. In racing, you're known to have been the first to start drafting on the superspeedways.

I don't think there's no question about it. I took a car to Daytona in 1960 that was about 10 or 15 miles an hour slower than the other cars that run the race and I won with drafting. That's the only way I won it. High-powered Pontiacs was factory backed and nobody was nowhere close to them. The Chevrolet I had was just so slow it wouldn't keep up. And the only way I could keep up was hang on to them.

How did you figure it out?

Fireball Roberts and Jack Smith was out playing around, running together and stuff. And they came by where I was at and I just lit in after them, you know, to see if I could run with them and stuff.

That was in practice?

In practice. Picked up their draft, it just set me right up there to them, and I just set there. And when I went back into the garage there, I told Ray Fox. Ray Fox was the mechanic on the car. I told Ray, 'I think I figured out a way to run with them guys.' And he said, 'How in the world are you going to do that?' I said, 'I don't know. When they came by a while ago I hooked onto them and they couldn't get away from me.'

And in the race?

All day long, that's all I did was hitch rides. If one of them went in the pits, I waited until another one come on. I just run, 'til another come on, I grabbed him and I rode him 'til he went in (the pits). And I just kept switching off. And when the thing was finally over with, I hitched enough rides 'til I had everybody beat.

After beating everybody on dirt, paved short tracks and superspeedways, you walked away from driving in NASCAR at the peak of your career. People don't do that very often.

I had pretty much made up my mind on what I was going to do when I got to where I didn't really have to

Above: *In 1981–82, Johnson and driver Darrell Waltrip won 24 races and two Winston Cups. Johnson was the first to emphasize tire stagger on cars downsized from wheelbases of 115 inches to 110.*

drive. And I kind of set a goal and when I reached that goal I had other opportunities to follow. Racing was a little bit of a hang up, me driving and owning cars, too. It tied me up so much I couldn't keep up with both of them and do other things I wanted to do. So I chose to own and operate the cars and do the other things too, because I had reached where I said I wanted to be in racing as a driver. And when I got there I just walked away from it. It's just that simple. I've never got back in a car since.

That's a reminder of the breakfast you once had with Bill France Sr., when he tried to convince you to go back to driving.
Well, he kept telling me that I was committed to racing. And I said, 'No, I'm not either.' And he said, 'Oh yeah you are.' I said, 'France you don't understand what being committed means.' Me and him was sitting down, eating breakfast when he said this to me. I said,

'For instance, if you sit down to breakfast and you have bacon and eggs, that chicken was involved, but that hog was committed.'

You've also had some pretty committed drivers in your equipment over the years and you always had high praise for Dale Earnhardt as well. What do you think set apart the guys who won championships for you like Cale Yarborough and Darrell Waltrip?
If a driver can only drive the car when it will drive itself, he's not really the race driver That's my way of looking at it. I've seen Dale Earnhardt, I've seen Cale Yarborough, Darrell Waltrip and them boys win races with cars that should have been put on the truck. And I've done it myself, so I know what I'm talking about. And when I see a driver that can only win a race when that car is absolutely perfect, as far as I'm concerned, then the car won the race, he didn't win. That's the way I see it.

Whiskey River

When the sun rose over Daytona Beach at the tranquil outset of the 1950s, stock car racing remained a defiant haven for bootlegging leadfoots, mechanically inclined farmers, roustabouts and adventurous men mustered out of the military.

Former B-17 bomber pilot Smokey Yunick, a mechanic, and the Flock brothers were typical. Bob, Fontello and Tim Flock all got their driver training delivering white whiskey around Atlanta.

The South's first high-banked superspeedway, Darlington Raceway, opened in 1950 and the crooked oval gave Bill France's series a call to arms versus the 500-mile race at Indianapolis. Plus, it helped overwhelm rival regional promoters like O. Bruton Smith and his National Stock Car Racing Association.

The biggest watershed had actually occurred a year before, when France re-introduced the concept of "Strictly Stock" cars in Charlotte. That race was designed to thwart Smith's Carolina-based series, not the last crossing of swords between the two men. Most of the 33 entrants drove their own cars to the June, 1949 event. Bob Flock started on the pole and a tobacco farmer named Lee Petty suffered the only

crash. Jim Roper of Kansas won in a Lincoln.

With big crowds at the inaugural races in Charlotte, then Darlington a year later and a non-points race at Atlanta's Lakewood Speedway, France and partners Ed Otto and Bill Tuthill knew they had a good thing going. France also had an iron hand on the controls. He disqualified the original Charlotte winner, Glenn Dunnaway, for welded springs on his 1947 Ford, an old bootleggers's trick. When the owner of Dunnaway's car sued, a judge determined France had the final say-so. Then, after Johnny Mantz of Los Angeles won the first Southern 500 the engine in his Plymouth, owned by France and Curtis Turner, went without inspection.

Other believers in stock cars were the factories. By 1956 Ford, Chrysler and Chevy had followed Hudson into NASCAR. This mixture of people, talent, machines and optimisim beat anything else in post-war America—outside of the Indy 500.

Previous page: *The 1953 Southern 500 featured 35 lead changes among pole winner Fonty Flock, Fireball Roberts, Herb Thomas and winner Buck Baker. Hudson driver Thomas, whose engine blew up while leading, won 12 races during the season and 12 poles plus his second straight championship. That's the No. 51 Olds of Gober Sosebee, another ace out of north Georgia.*

Above: *Despite its wobbling front wheel, Bob Flock's Olds leads the Ford of Joe Jernigan and the Lincoln of Lloyd Moore through the south turn of the Beach & Road Course in 1950. Attendance was estimated at 9,500. It would be three more years before Bill France proposed a track be built in Daytona to handle increasing crowds.*

Left: *After moving up from wheelman, France usually allowed drivers to continue using fenders and then fists to enforce rules on the track. In the mid-1950s, the factories began building cars specifically for NASCAR racing, which also created rules issues. Then, after a young fan was killed by a crash at Martinsville, Va. in 1957, the factories abruptly withdrew, creating another headache.*

Right: *Sen. Strom Thurmond and his wife greet Mildred and Harold Brasington (setting down flower box) at the first Southern 500. Bill France had tried to persuade Brasington to build a superspeedway in Hillsborough, N.C., where France owned a short track. France then offered to co-sanction Darlington's 500-mile event with the Carolina States Racing Association, affiliated with Brasington. A pivotal move, it prevented Sam Nunis from running the South's first 500-miler on Atlanta's Lakewood Speedway.*

Below: *Red Vogt, the godfather of all NASCAR mechanics, stands next to Raymond Parks' 1939 Ford. Such "modifieds" carried stock car racing after the war until NASCAR created the "Strictly Stock" division. Parks owned the Olds Red Byron drove to the first "Strictly Stock" title in 1949.*

Above: The "Flying Mile" was a major feature of the February beach race meetings, a holdover from the era of land speed record attempts. Tim Flock, with the help of the camera lens, has a Lincoln that appears to "fly." Julius Timothy Flock was also fond of stretching the truth with colorful tales. "My mother Maudie would cross fingers on her left hand if I was racing," went one story. "If Bob was running, she'd cross her right fingers. And cross her ankles if Fonty was running. She'd sit like that from 2 o'clock until we called home and tell her what we'd done."

Left: "Miss Martha," Flock's 1951 Lincoln, was a big car with a big engine, typical of the Grand National division—the name given to the "Strictly Stock" category in 1950. Once behind the hemi engine of a Chrysler C-300, the talented Flock won a record 18 races, 18 poles and the championship in 1955.

Above: The Hudsons of Fonty Flock (14), Joe Eubanks (82) and Dick Rathmann (120) swept the front row at Darlington in 1953, but were paced by a Nash, another small company trying to sustain itself. The Hudsons were powered by 308-cubic inch, side valve six-cylinders that produced massive torque compared to Olds' overhead valve V-8. Buck Baker won the race in an Olds.

Whiskey River

Above: Car owner Raymond Parks changes a tire on his Cadillac entry in the first Southern 500 en route to third place. Note the air wrenches and Parks' immaculate dress as well as the torn up tire, a common problem that day. The first "Strictly Stock" champion, Parks' driver Red Byron, left the Grand Nationals after NASCAR stripped him of his 1950 points for competing in a rival series. Strong-arm tactics were also typical of France's rival, the AAA Contest Board, which used similar methods to keep its Indy car and stock car drivers loyal.

Left: Fonty Flock exits the north turn in Daytona. The co-driver of his Olds is a stuffed monkey. Brother Tim later raced with a real one and Fonty gained notoriety by wearing "Bermooda shorts" while competing.

Above: Lee Petty won his first championship in 1954 driving a Chrysler. Petty was the runner-up to Red Byron and car owner Raymond Parks' Olds in the 1949 "Strictly Stock" season. He would have won the title the following year over Bill Rexford had he not been stripped of points at mid-season by Bill France for driving in events not sanctioned by NASCAR. Here, short track champion Jim Reed (left) joins France and Petty at the 1954 awards banquet.

Left: Mechanic/driver Jack Smith won a race or a pole every year from 1956 though 1964. He could win on dirt short tracks as well as superspeedways, recording 21 victories and 24 poles. Pictured after winning on dirt at Martinsville, Va. in 1956, Smith thought he could have been a bigger star had he not driven his own cars and been "such a hard ass."

Opposite page: Tim (40 career Grand National wins), left, and Fonty Flock (19 wins) smiled and joked much more than older brother Bob, who grew particularly grim after breaking his back in a crash a second time following four career victories.

Above: Frank "Rebel" Mundy won the AAA title in 1955 driving for Carl Kiekhaefer. Late in 1955, NASCAR's political power was enhanced when the AAA withdrew from racing. Indianapolis Motor Speedway owner Tony Hulman then started the United States Auto Club.

Right: Tim Flock in happier times driving a Hudson. Flock's Chrysler days with the Kiekhaefer team did not last long; he quit early in the 1956 season due to ulcers but raced until banned in 1961. He won 21 percent of his races (40 victories in 189 starts), still the all-time best.

Opposite page from top: Former bus driver Buck Baker was hired by Carl Kiekhaefer to drive Chrysler C-300's in 1956 with the immortal words: "If you're as tough an s.o.b. as everybody says, I want to hire you." Baker's 46th and last win came in the Southern 500 at age 45. Herb Thomas (bottom) and mechanic Smokey Yunick helped introduce the small block Chevy V-8 in 1955 and were part of the factory team known as "The Hot Ones."

Right: *Carl Kiekhaefer was the first multi-car team owner and the first to utilize major corporate sponsorship—his own Mercury Outboard Motors company. At Daytona in 1956, Tim Flock drove a new Chrysler 300-B from the pole to victory. Behind him came reinforcements: Buck Baker (No. 301) in a year old C-300, Fonty Flock (No. 500-B) in a new Dodge D-500, Frank "Rebel" Mundy (No. 300-B) in a new Chrysler and black driver Charlie Scott in a year-old C-300 (following Mundy).*

Kiekhaefer was the first to transport race cars in large trucks and to outfit his team in uniforms. A mechanical genius, the Wisconsinite was also a stern taskmaster. "You're fired!" he said to crew members. "But you can't leave until the car is ready."

A friend of Walter Chrysler, Kiekhaefer encouraged and aided the development of a special 300-horsepower hemi engine with dual four-barrel carburetors, special cams and crankshafts. Flock won at Daytona in 1955 despite an automatic transmission. (Fireball Roberts was disqualified from first for a 16/1000ths variance in his Pontiac's pushrod as Bill France sought to encourage Chrysler.)

Kiekhaefer eventually became a headache, because his cars won so often. After Flock won the Grand National title in 1955, Baker won it the following year and Mundy won the AAA title in 1955. The team won 22 of the first 29 NASCAR races in 1956, including one string of 16 straight. Fans began to boo and throw bottles at the rich man's cars.

After 1956, Kiekhaefer abruptly left. Ironically, when he switched Mercury's emphasis to four-cycle inboard boat engines, he didn't choose Chrysler. Instead, Kiehaefer bought thousands of engines each year from Chevy!

Above: Carl Kiekhaefer hired Herb Thomas (second from left) to replace the departed Tim Flock in 1956. Thomas defected after 29 races, returning with his own Chevrolet. That set up a fateful race in Shelby, N.C., added to the schedule late in the season by Kiekaefer, who had rented the facility and got a NASCAR sanction from Bill France. With Buck Baker (third from left) closing on Thomas in the points race, Speedy Thompson (far right) turned Thomas's Chevy into the wall, starting a massive pile-up. The all-time victory leader in the Grand Nationals at the time with 48 wins, Thomas never won another race after suffering a head injury. Smokey Yunick, who kept Kiekaefer's photo framed by a toilet seat on the wall of his garage, blamed team tactics.

Left: Lee Petty switched to Dodge from Chrysler in 1956, then won his two titles in 1958–59 aboard Oldsmobiles.

Above: *Glenn "Fireball" Roberts catapulted to superstar status in 1958 due to his capacity for high speed and the changing times. In June of 1957, America's factories had formally agreed to withdraw from racing after a young boy was killed by Billy Myers' crash at Martinsville, Va. That left many regular stars stranded. Roberts, meanwhile, had given up running full-time in the much faster modified ranks to come back to the Grand Nationals. In 1958, he lapped the field each time to win on all three tracks of one mile or longer in Trenton, N.J., Raleigh, N.C. and Darlington, S.C. aboard a Frank Strickland-owned Chevy.*

Right: "Ronda (N.C.) Roadrunner" Junior Johnson returned to action in 1958 to win six races after serving a prison sentence in Chillicothe, O., including both events at his home track in North Wilkesboro and one skein of three straight.

Below: Billy Meyers, the 1955 Late Model Sportsman champion, on the beach in a Mercury. Later in 1958, Myers died of a heart attack while leading a modified race in Winston-Salem, N.C. The year before, brother Bobby Myers fatally collided with Fonty Flock in the Southern 500, which also ended Flock's driving career.

Opposite page: Ralph Earnhardt made several attempts at the Grand Nationals, but despite leading some events usually found hard luck instead. So he remained a bigger fish on the weekly short track circuit and won the 1956 Late Model Sportsman championship. Earnhardt's exploits included winning 17 straight times at the Hickory, N.C. track.

Richard Petty

People began referring to seven-time champion Richard Petty as "The King" long before he began ruling the record book. His bearing, as much as his driving, helped bring him that regal respect. The statistics are in his favor as well. He scored the most wins (200) in NASCAR's premier division, started the most races (1,177), scored the most short tracks poles (97) and the most over-all (126). None of those records are likely to be broken and he certainly will be the career leader for most wins in a season (27), most consecutive wins (10) and most Daytona 500 wins (7) among many other milestones.

Did you envision the impact the Daytona International Speedway was going to have on NASCAR racing when it opened in 1959?

Even coming down to Daytona and running on the beach was a big thing, because it opened the season. But it was just another race once the season got started. When the track first opened up, we looked at it the same way. Darlington was the track at that particular time, ever since the 1950s. The finish with Daddy and Beauchamp, that pretty much put Daytona on the map. There wasn't that much newspaper and radio coverage. But what did cover it really put it out there for three or four days after the race. They got more publicity after the race than before the race.

What do you recall about those three days that NASCAR took to decide before it was declared Lee Petty had won what became a photo finish with Johnny Beauchamp?

It was hurry up and wait. In our hearts, we won the race. But the deal was, was France going to change his mind? We'd worked with him for ten years so we was used to what he said was law. He wanted the Thunderbird to win because he wanted Ford to get back into racing. He had an alternative motive, not that he was against Lee Petty, but it would be better if a

Ford won because it might get them back interested. The kickback from the press, the people who had pictures and people who had seen the actual finish, after a while the judgment come out that forget about (the Ford), I've got to make this deal work.

Two years later, your father had a terrible crash here during a qualifying race when his car went over the old steel guard rail and left the track. How concerned were you that he wasn't going to survive?

I was real concerned until I got to the hospital and seen him. Even though he had a punctured lung, his leg was all tore up, his ribs broke and stuff. When I got there and he was breathing, I knowed he was going to be OK, because I knowed how hard-headed he was. That was the end of his career and took me to the forefront. At that time, he stayed down here for four months. He told us, 'OK, now get ready for the next race.' We didn't have any sponsors. We was racing out of our mother's pocket book. She kept all the bills and had all the money. She stayed down here with him. Up until that time my brother (Maurice) and I were doing all the work that Daddy said to get done. All of a sudden we were doing everything. We had to do the work, write the checks and do everything. We grew up

Above: *The Pettys had run Chrysler products since 1949 with few exceptions. But when Richard Petty switched to GM in 1979, the ads suggested it was a natural pairing, touting "baseball, apple pie, Richard Petty and Chevrolet."*

right quick. I was 23 years old and all of a sudden Petty racing was put on our shoulders.

The Plymouths were underpowered during the 1962 and 1963 seasons. Is that the reason why you began to run the high lines on various race tracks, and did you start doing that at Daytona?
It was as much at Daytona as anywhere. The old Plymouths could handle great, but you had to keep them wound up with enough horsepower to get you out of the corners. We didn't have that. We had to run off the bank to keep the thing running. I came to Daytona as rookie in 1959 with a convertible. Junior Johnson, Fireball Roberts and Daddy and everybody

else came here as rookies, too. They didn't have any more experience than I did. I was just startin'. I had run ten or 12 races the year before. I didn't have to unlearn to learn anything. Every time I made a lap I learned. I didn't have to forget what I knew and then do it all over again. It was a really good time in my career to start at Daytona. That's what made Richard Petty as far as getting his name out there.

Once you got the hemi in 1964, you won your first Daytona 500. The speeds were up considerably due to the effectiveness of the new Dodge engine with its hemispherical combustion chambers. Was that a white-knuckle race for you?

Above: *With the factories gone again, Petty Enterprises dominated with the parts left over from Chrysler. Driving Plymouths and Dodges, Petty won four championships in the five seasons from 1971–75.*

Not really, we were just faster than everybody else. If you drove a Plymouth, you probably had more experience than some of those who had been running up front. I had been running in the pack for a couple of years and had to figure out how to get around somebody who was quicker than me. I probably wound up developing more of my drafting skills. When we did get enough go to go, we knew what it took to get around the race track. When you take a car with no power and get it to run pretty good, when you did get the power you said, 'OK, that's the faster way around and that's the way to go.'

The cars were pretty close to stock at that time. So you really had to work at driving.

In 1964, they had gotten away from stock in the suspension, springs and shocks. They had modified stock stuff and it was really beginning to be racing stuff as far as underneath. The bodies were stock. They had doors that opened and shut and windows that rolled

up and down, you had a bank seat in the front and took one side of the bench out. You had to have all the door panels and hood panels and that kind of stuff in them. They weren't easy to drive. The cars didn't handle as good, they had small narrow tires, no spoilers, so if you had a Plymouth, it was pretty much stock. It had chrome on it. You just stopped up the headlights. It had to look stock.

Would some of the guys from the 1990s have had trouble driving cars like that?

If you take the guys (from the 1990s) and put them in those cars, there wouldn't be two or three that would have made it in those cars. Even guys back then like Bobby Allison and Dave Marcis were not very big, but they were wiry, you know what I mean? Maybe the guys back then weren't in that good of shape as guys that came along later, but they were in shape to drive a race car. If some of the modern guys went back, they couldn't have made it in those cars. But if they had come up at that time, most of them probably could have done it.

The hemi got outlawed in the 1965 season by NASCAR. How much did you guys get involved in the politics at that time?

We had nothing to say about it. Naturally we wanted to go racing. The factories had a little more pull than we did. We got into a situation (with Chrysler) where NASCAR said it's our rules and if you want to play that's fine. All three manufacturers are in it again, but they're (still) playing more under NASCAR rules than what they want.

When Chrysler boycotted the first half of the 1965 season, Petty Enterprises maintained its relationship with the factory and racing by going drag racing with a Plymouth Barracuda. How much did if affect you when you had the accident at a Georgia drag strip, where your car went into the crowd and killed a little boy?

That was really, really a low point. You didn't want to be drag racing in the first place, because you wanted to be going 'round and 'round. But by having kids, the whole family deal and getting into the accident, that was probably the hardest part of my whole career. It was sort of downer anyway, because you weren't doing what you wanted to do. And then when something like that happens, it's just really bad. It was probably my most emotional time, to still go forward and still have that on your mind. But you had to go. You had too many people working for you and too many responsibilities that you couldn't just sit back and say, 'OK forget it.'

The rules were changed for 1966 and NASCAR allowed the hemi engines to compete with 405 cubic inches instead of 426. You came back to Daytona and won the 500 after lapping the field. That must have been a big moment for you.

We were still able to dominate the race. A lot of people had the hemi, too, and we still had a better combination. We had run 14 races in the latter part of 1965 (when NASCAR first relaxed the rules). We got back into the groove, but we only raced at one big track at Rockingham. We missed Atlanta. At that time we come down to Daytona three weeks ahead to qualify and then for a week we didn't do nothing, except go out and run and work on the race car.

The 1967 season was certainly extraordinary, when you won 27 races and ten straight at one point driving the Petty Enterprises Plymouth.

We didn't run that good at Daytona and then went out and won some short track races every three or four weeks, on the average of what we had been doin'. Then all of a sudden it just hit and we won everything for what—two or three months? We weren't doing anything any different and we just kept on doing it and fate just stepped in. The odds evened up and we had a super good year.

Did the ten straight victories in 1967 change your life? It was a celebrated sports story at the time.

The ten straight came about because you ran two or three times a week. When you finished the race, the most important thing was the next race, whether you run last or first. If we won a race, we wasn't settled in on that; I mean we were thinking where's the next race track? We've got to go home and get this car ready. You didn't have but one car and ran the same car everywhere you went.

A Firestone tire representative from that era says that tire temperatures clearly indicated Petty Enterprises had figured out how to use left side weight better than anybody else. How much was Chrysler involved?

We just did our own thing. At that time Chrysler was not totally involved. Chrysler was working with a team owner out of Indiana, near Chicago. We were down in North Carolina doing our own thing. They came with their hubs and axles and springs, but we made it work.

What was your most memorable race during the recording breaking 1967 season?

In Nashville one night we got behind by about 12 laps and still won by four laps. That was circumstances beyond our control. We run into the wall due to tires or something and tore the back end off the car. They just lined it up by eyesight and we went and won the race because everybody else had trouble. Not that we outrun 'em that much, you know what I mean? We made the laps up when the leaders fell out. It was one of those races where you just run and run and run and whoever was there at the end won. We survived. Back then you had to do a little figurin'. 'OK, you can only run so hard because the tires would only stand so much or the car will only stand so much.' The drivers had to do a lot more figurin' and were involved more in the race part and not spend all their time doing nothin' but driving the car. It was just a different era. Before the race, the driver and crew had to figure what kind of equipment they had and who you had to race.

Did your nickname of "King Richard" come out of the 1967 season?
Somewhere along in that era. Three or four of the writers who went to all the races, I think they was all out drinking one night and that's how they come up with it (laughter). Once it's written two or three times, the next guy picked it up and so on. I don't think it would have happened if I had been named Joe.

How much did your responsibilities as a star in motor racing contribute to the fact later in your career that you developed ulcers and had to undergo surgery to have the upper portion of your stomach removed?
I think it had more to do with your habits and the way you eat than the pressures. Any pressures you had on you was in the way you dieted and the way you ate and slept. As far as that causing ulcers. We finally figured out that that's going to cause ulcers. It was just a deal of being totally consumed with racing. That's what consumed you. If you had time to eat you did, and if you didn't, you didn't. More than the pressure mentally, it was just a physical deal.

You seemed to enjoy the role of being the guy people looked to as the leader in the sport.
It's always more enjoyable to be on top. It's not any easier, but it was a lot more enjoyable. You could do something and then go out and copy something. You got results at that particular time instead of having to work, work, work and wait ten years.

One of the most unique aspects of NASCAR history was when the Professional Drivers Association came about and there was a driver's strike at Talladega. How much of it had to do with purses being paid at that time?

My side of the story is this. Back then promoters would pay (the better teams) appearance money under the table to get you to come to the race. We went to all of them and we got our cut. Talladega had just opened up and a lot of the drivers were concerned with the safety and how the drivers were treated at the tracks by NASCAR and the race tracks per se, and also the purses. But we never got into the purse deal. We said lets look at the convenience for our families when we get to the racetrack, and the safety. I told the guys, 'Look I don't need no part of this. I'm on top of this deal, I'm makin' more money out of it than anybody, I'm getting my deal money. So why should I be involved?' They said, 'For it to happen, we need to have everybody involved.' I said OK. Well, me and Bobby (Allison) got caught with it. We were doing the best at that time and we thought we could help somebody else and we wound up taking the blunt end of it. I don't regret doing it, I just regret the way they did do it. The deal was we went to Michigan right before Talladega and started the (PDA) there. We got to Talladega and they were having all kinds of trouble with the tires. So that was the organization, the beginning and the end of it at one time. We never got to present any of our problems to NASCAR or any of the tracks or any of that stuff. The Talladega deal came up and everybody said, 'We're an organization and we ain't going to run.' I was the head leader of it and they tell me what they wanted to do and I said, 'OK if that's what you all want to do, then that's what we'll do.'

And then after the race was run without any regulars other than Bobby Isaac, it seemed like the PDA lost all its leverage.
What happened then, everybody went home and they run the race. Before they had any more races, the track owners and NASCAR got together and said, 'OK, we'll start paying these people a little something to show up.' That's where the car owner points deals come up, where everybody starts getting a little bit of the deal (to show up). In all groups of people, you've still got individuals. So when the tracks started talking to these guys about giving them a couple of bucks to come to the races, there went your organization. They went and picked the organization apart by going to the individuals. Which was good in the long run. It was

Above: *In the 1970s, "The King" began wearing crowns consisting of a cowboy hat with feathers, invariably given away to charity auctions. Dark glasses were present from his earliest days.*

better. I don't want nobody organizing against my business and basically that's what they was lookin' at, that we was organizing against their business. We was wantin' a say in it, OK? We never got that far along.

What about all the drivers you ran against. Was David Pearson the best?
He was the best all-around driver I ever run against. He could run on short dirt, short asphalt, big dirt, big asphalt, it didn't make any difference. When he had a decent car, he was the guy to beat. A lot of guys that come through are just good on road courses or superspeedways. He was good on all of them.

Were you better than David, or was he better than you?
When they had the top 50 in the 50 years of NASCAR history, you never seen me on top of anybody's list as being a good driver. The only list I was on was I won more than anybody else. That was all I was interested in. I was never interested in being the best at anything other than being the best winner. The bottom line, you know what I mean? What is your criteria to say whose better than anybody else? There's no way you can say whose the fastest gun. Different eras, different circumstances, the whole deal.

That's true, but your opinion means a lot.
I would put David up against anybody any time in any circumstances. That's not taking anything away from Cale Yarborough or Bobby Allison, because they were good, too.

When the factories stopped racing, you won three out of four Daytona 500s.
When the factories pulled out in '70 and we still have all that Chrysler stuff. So we run in '71 and '72 and then we run out of all that stuff. In '72, we hung in with STP. We were the first people to have a nationally known sponsor. Then I guess Purolator came on next with the Wood Brothers.

At that time, were you worried about the future of the sport and the lack of sponsorship for most teams given that the factories had pulled out?
We lived through the deal of '57 when all the factories were in it and then '58 and all the factories pulled out. Everybody ran '57 cars in '58. And '59 was the same. There was not that much money. It was a low ebb in '57 and in '70 when everybody pulled out, people said there's going to be a backlash. People are not going to be putting money in it. We got fortunate to hang on to STP and get that started and other people then seen this was a viable venture. Then you had national sponsors come in with $250,000 or $300,000 at a time. All of sudden you've got $250,000 with a contract with a sponsor. That was a bunch of money when the year before you didn't have nothin'.

R.J. Reynolds Tobacco Co. got involved at that time as well and the Grand National series became known as the Winston Cup. What effect did R.J. Reynolds' corporate and financial involvement have in turning things around?
They got started in '71. That year we run 47 or 48 races. In '72 they cut it back down to 31 races. Then we started runnin' bigger venues and did away with the dirt and started runnin' bigger, longer races. The longer races naturally paid more money, so you had a better chance of makin' a livin' out of it. The France family needed help, too. The tracks needed help, NASCAR needed help to deal with the tracks and join up with them. What they done was organize it a whole lot better.

43

Richard Petty

1959-71

Factory Feuds

Like much of life elsewhere, experimentation, upheaval and the media's coverage of it drove NASCAR in the 1960's as much as the grand vision of Bill France's new Daytona International Speedway. Starting with the big tracks in Atlanta and Charlotte, a slew of superspeedways followed the successful launch of Daytona, amply aided by the controversial finish of the first Daytona 500 in 1959.

The live and let live spirit of the decade spilled into the corporate boardrooms in Detroit, which financed factory teams and outrageous machinery, culminating in 1969 with the Dodge Daytona and the Plymouth Superbird. Equipped with 426-inch displacement hemi engines, dual four-barrel carburetors and strut-mounted wings in the rear, these street legal muscle cars needed only a 19-inch front bumper section added to balance the aerodynamics for the banked tracks. These were responses to Ford's fastback Torino and the company's single overhead cam 427 V-8's as well as Chevy's stagger valve or "porcupine" head.

The Ford and Chrysler factories leaned hard on France to get their special engines and cars approved. General Motors, meanwhile, occasionally pipped their efforts by financing the skunkworks on the Halifax River in Daytona run by Smokey Yunick, a true mechanical mastermind and thorn in the rule makers' side, while Ralph Moody pioneered the tube-frame roll cage.

But the currents of speed and change brought with them a heavy price. Curtis Turner and Tim Flock were banned by France for seeking financing for the Charlotte track from the Teamsters Union. Fireball Roberts died in a fiery crash at Charlotte in 1964. But it was the horrid wire service photos of Don MacTavish's fatal accident at Daytona in 1969 that depicted doom for the the factories, already under pressure from Congress and the insurance industry to put more emphasis on safety. Within two years, the factories were gone.

Left: *Beauchamp went to Victory Lane, said the Pettys, because France was trying to lure Ford into the world of NASCAR.*

Above: *T. Taylor Warren's decisive photograph shows Lee Petty's Olds (in middle) beating Johnny Beauchamp's Ford (at bottom) as they catch a lapped car at the finish of the first Daytona 500.*

Right: *France milked three days of publicity while searching for additional evidence before handing the trophy to Petty. Warren was the track photographer and had produced the "photo finish" shortly after the race.*

Previous page: *Bobby Isaac, winner of 37 career races and 51 poles, and Curtis Turner.*

Factory Feuds

Above: Despite all the roaring headlines on the big tracks, NASCAR continued running dirt tracks until 1970. Junior Johnson tied Rex White for most victories in 1959 with his fifth win, taken from the pole at Hickory, N.C.

Above: Atlanta opened one of three banked superspeedways built in 1960. The others were in Charlotte and in Hanford, Calif. Fireball Roberts won the inaugural Dixie 300 in Atlanta.

Above: Glenn Wood won three Grand National events in 1960, but was best known as founder of the Wood Brothers team.

Above: *The son of a moonshiner who saved enough money bootlegging to buy saw mills, Curtis Turner's dirt track technique was unsurpassed. A party-throwing womanizer, Turner loved being in the middle of the action on or off the track. Nicknamed "Pops" for his fondness for banging doors, the playboy always tried to talk his way out of the fist fights.*

Factory Feuds

Left: Ned Jarrett, left, won with gritty consistency and was a teetotaling fundamentalist. Practical joker Joe Weatherly, also a two-time champion, once filled the water jug in the race car of friend Curtis Turner with bourbon.

Right: Lee Petty' knocks down the guard rail during a qualifying race at Daytona in 1961 after locking bumpers with Johnny Beauchamp, who follows him over. The two principals of the famed '59 finish were again in a tight battle on the final lap when the crash occurred. It ended the careers of both.

Below: Winner David Pearson (left) overtakes the Chevy of 1960 Grand National champion Rex White in Atlanta in 1961.

Right: *Frederick Christian "Fast Freddy" Lorenzen of Elmhurst, Ill., became the first Golden Boy of NASCAR. Blond, handsome, fast and cocky, the Yankee was a meticulous perfectionist and hothead, but knew how to celebrate after victories.*

This party occurred in Atlanta in 1962, shortly after he joined the Hulman-Moody factory team. Note the "Competition Proven" legend on Lorenzen's shirt (even though most of Ford's racing equipment at the time was not available to the public).

When Lorenzen won his first superspeedway race in 1961 at Darlington, he cried. He followed exploits at the track on the radio in a tent pitched in his backyard while growing up. As was his custom, leader Turner repeatedly chopped Lorenzen's faster Ford that day and tried to put him into the outside wall. Lorenzen made a late pass on the inside to beat Turner, who later slammed into the upstart's car in the pits.

His speaking ability and his handsome image made Lorenzen the perfect candidate to lead Ford's public relations campaign and helped promote the image of stock car racing in general. The factory team concentrated on the superspeedway events and Lorenzen never won a championship, considered less important than money winnings and 500-mile victories at the time. Lorenzen scored 12 superspeedway victories in seven seasons with Holman-Moody and at least one 500-mile victory in each season from 1962–66.

In a typically impulsive decision, Lorenzen retired to the real estate business after crashing in Atlanta in the spring of 1967. A later comeback attempt failed.

Above: NASCAR raced whenever possible in the 1960s to thwart competition, particularly from the United States Auto Club, formed by Indianapolis Motor Speedway owner Tony Hulman. The lone race in November of 1963 at the Augusta International Raceway road course produced the last victory of Fireball Roberts (No. 22).

Left: Fish camp owner DeWayne "Tiny" Lund, overlooked for a factory ride, saved Marvin Panch from a burning Maserati in a preliminary race at Daytona in 1963. Lund then won the 500 after substituting for Panch in the Wood Brothers' Ford. His accident at Talladega in 1975 proved fatal.

Right: In the midst of F-1 and Indy fame, Dan Gurney's crossover ability and his familiarity with Riverside, Calif.'s road course brought him five Grand National victories from 1963–68.

Above: *Wendell Scott, a bootlegger from Danville, Va., was admired by many of his fellow drivers for his driving skill, mechanical ingenuity and calm tenacity in the face of constant racism. It wasn't by chance he won a race in Jacksonville, Fla., in 1964. Like many of his fellow independents, Scott was often hard-pressed to keep racing due to budget constraints. He hung new bodies on former factory Fords to keep them eligible and finished in the top ten in the points three times.*

Left: Fireball Roberts' nickname came from his days as a Florida State baseball pitcher, which helped sportswriters begin recognizing drivers as athletes. When the superspeedway boom hit in the 1960s, Roberts was in his element. He scored a record five 500-mile victories and 14 superspeedway triumphs. According to friends, Roberts had lost his edge and was contemplating retirement due to nerves frayed by the constant tire failures on the banked tracks during his hey day. But his fatal accident resulted when his car was collected after Ned Jarrett and Junior Johnson collided on the seventh lap of the 1964 World 600 in Charlotte. He died from burns a month later.

Right: Considered by some a better practical joker than race car driver, Weatherly's back-to-back championships in 1962 (in a Ford owned by Bud Moore) and 1963 (in a Mercury owned by the Wood Brothers) resulted from consistency in an era where the season often included more than 50 races. Little Joe died early in 1964 from a relatively minor accident in the esses at Riverside, Calif., because he thought it was safer to wear his shoulder harness loosely.

Above: *Four years after his ban from NASCAR, Curtis Turner reappeared in Victory Lane for the first time at Rockingham.
"Another party's startin' in 'bout 15 minutes," he said, as usual. A spectacular crash in Atlanta in 1967 forced Turner into
retirement. Turner died three years later after a crash in his private plane in Pennsylvania.*

Above: *Curtis Turner and Bruton Smith, shown here at the first World 600 in 1960, became uneasy partners in the building of the Charlotte Motor Speedway. Granite had unexpectedly increased construction costs. The duo required a shotgun and a pistol to keep unpaid, rebellious workers from sabotaging the paving. When Turner sought to borrow $850,000 from the Teamsters Union, Bill France banned him and Tim Flock for joining the Federation of Professional Athletes and trying to recruit other drivers. Turner and Smith, meanwhile, lost the track during bankruptcy. Smith returned to reclaim it in 1975 by quietly buying up the stock.*

Left: *Richard Petty became the first two-time winner at the Daytona 500 in 1966, joyously returning after Chrysler's boycott.*

Factory Feuds

Left: *Driving an experimental Holman-Moody chassis that careened wildly in the corners, Mario Andretti scored his first major victory in the 1967 Daytona 500. Ford execs ordered Andretti to be held in the pits to boost Lorenzen's chances.*

Below: *Richard Petty's incredible 27-win season in 1967 was mostly a short track affair. Petty drove his Plymouth to a record ten straight victories starting at Bowman Gray's flat quarter mile.*

Opposite page (top): *The Mercury Cyclone helped Cale Yarborough beat David Pearson in the 1968 Southern 500 and Lee Roy Yarbrough in the Daytona 500. The best of the early streamliners led to aero wars and templates from NASCAR.*

Opposite page (bottom): *NASCAR banned Smokey Yunick's 1968 Chevelle, but the legend is incorrect. It did not measure ⅞ths of legal size (the bodywork had simply been moved). Nor did he drive away from the inspectors without a fuel tank or fuel (by his account, he added fuel).*

Right: In the upheaval over rules regarding the big block engines, NASCAR's compromise for the 1966 season included an option for smaller, mid-size sedans. This introduced the 115-inch wheelbase cars that would eventually rule the roost, because they were allowed to carry the big block engines along with a weight penalty for those sized above 405 cubic inches. This gave the racers the best of both worlds: more horsepower and smaller cars. At this stage, Ford's engineers began working on aerodynamically slick cars to help overcome the weight penalty. Not everybody was on the same page. Petty Engineering decided the blocky mid-size Plymouth Belvedere at 405 cubic inches for the hemi V-8 got the best results on the big track when it came to power versus weight and handling. That's the car that gave Richard Petty victory in the 1966 Daytona 500 from the pole (at 175.165 mph).

Seemingly always one step ahead, Smokey Yunick's 1967 Chevelle, with aerodynamics sculpted top and bottom from a clunky mid-size Chevy, won the Daytona pole the next year (180.831 mph), also with a 405 cubic inch Chevy engine (and under-the-table factory help). But Ford's focus on aerodynamics began to pay handsomely in 1968 with the Mercury Cyclone and Ford Torino. They took the added weight penalty and still blew away the competition. The fastbacks were so quick Petty wanted the new Dodge Charger instead of a Plymouth for 1969. The factory said no, so he left Chrysler to campaign a Torino Cobra in 1969.

Petty's judgement about the Dodge proved accurate. Bobby Isaac went on to win 19 races with the Charger that year.

In this photo, Petty, who won ten races for Ford, rides alongside David Pearson in Atlanta.

Above: Buddy Baker, in a test session at Talladega in March of 1970, drove the Dodge Daytona to the first recorded lap over 200 mph by a Grand National stock car. Bobby Isaac, that year's champion, then raised the record to 201.104 mph.

Left: Jim Hurtubise, burned in a 1964 Indy Car accident, had surgical repairs to his hands that allowed him to grip a steering wheel. He won in Atlanta in 1966, beating Fred Lorenzen by a lap.

Opposite page: Lee Roy Yarbrough (left) gave Donnie Allison the relief driving needed for car owner Banjo Matthews (center) to win the World 600. Matthews became the predominant car builder in NASCAR during the 1970's. His nickname came from the shape of the frames of gold-rimmed glasses worn when he ran modifieds on the beach in Daytona.

Factory Feuds

Left: *John Holman was the perfect guy to run a team for a factory, but did not get the same appreciation drivers had for his partner Ralph Moody, a former midget driver in New England who migrated to stock cars and Florida after the war.*

Behind Moody are the Ford factory drivers of 1965: Fred Lorenzen, A.J. Foyt, Curtis Turner, Junior Johnson, Ned Jarrett, Marvin Panch, Dick Hutcherson and Cale Yarborough. (Moody's children are seated next to him.)

John Holman bought the parts inventory of the Ford factory team when they withdrew the first time from NASCAR in 1957 under a covenant drawn by the Automobile Manufacturers' Association, which banned participation in racing. Holman took one of his drivers, Moody, as a partner.

Ford knew the value of its performance image and maintained unofficial contact with Holman, busy selling Ford race cars and parts to customers. When Henry Ford II ordered his company back into racing in 1962, Holman-Moody emerged as an official factory entrant.

Holman succeeded in part because he gave the Ford executives free rein to make racing decisions. But Moody did not always play the corporate game. Holman attempted to fire Moody and his crew during the 1963 Rebel 400 at Darlington because Moody refused an order from executive Jacques Passino about tire and race strategy. Fred Lorenzen and Fireball Roberts finished one-two thanks to Moody. Not surprisingly, once the factory pulled out a second time in 1971, the Holman and Moody partnership collapsed due to legal issues.

Cale Yarborough

Cale Yarborough perfected the concept of winning the Winston Cup by relentless pursuit. In 1976-78, a time when Winston's sponsorship had brought more prestige and money to the points title, Yarborough became the first driver to capture three straight championships. During that span, the blond bantamweight won 28 of 90 races, 13 poles and led an incredible 10,508 laps.

You grew up not far from the Darlington Raceway in Timmonsville, South Carolina. If you hadn't grown up so close to the track, would you have ever started racing?
Well, you never know. But it played a major role.

You saw your first races at the track as a boy?
I would crawl under the fence during the race and they'd catch me and throw me out. Then I'd climb over the fence to get in and they'd catch me and throw me out again.

And you drove your first race at Darlington in 1957 as a teenager, after lying about your age.
I ran my first race there when I was 17 years old. There were some people who put up some money and had a car. You had to be 21 at the time to get a license. I had a hard time making my first one, but I didn't give up on it. I went on to win five Southern 500s. Nobody else has won five Southern 500s.

Was it an eye opener for you that first race?
I thought I was a pro at that time. It didn't take me long to find out that people like Fireball Roberts were way ahead of me. I'd had a couple of years of dirt track under my belt, and I really thought I was a race driver. I thought I'd make Buck Baker and Fireball and all those boys stand back and take notice. I found out that I wasn't ready to carry their helmet bag. I was going to need a lot of experience to run with those guys.

The biggest break you got in your career was in a race at the Asheville-Weaverville Speedway in North Carolina in 1963, when Ford's Jacques Passino gave you and Benny Parsons cars in a tryout to see who would be chosen as a Ford factory driver. What do you recall about the pressure at that time?
It was a lot of pressure. That was going to be my major break if it worked out, you know. I put all the effort I could in to making it happen. I kind of felt badly for Benny, but I had to look out for myself. Of course in the end Benny went on to do well, too. I ran good, ran up front, ran strong. And Benny had some problems. And so when it was over, they said I had the job. If I had lost, it would have been cruel as hell. I really don't know if I'd have stayed in the racing business or not.

What were the fellows from Ford and Detroit like when it came to running a team in the South?
They were all professional people. They were dedicated to making Ford's presence known in NASCAR. They were all business, especially Jacques Passino. I can remember him telling me one day, 'I don't care how many fenders is on that car, I don't care whether it's upside down, I don't care what kind of condition it's in—as long as you were in front when it happened.' I never forgot that and I made it a point to always run up front if there was any possible way. That's the way he wanted it and that's the way he got it.

Above: *Twenty years after lying about his age to drive in the Southern 500, Yarborough won the 1976 Winston Cup championship. Patti Huffman, the Miss Winston that year, later became Kyle Petty's wife.*

Once the factories withdrew from NASCAR you tried the Indy cars with some success. Was it inevitable that you would eventually come back to the stock cars?
Well, yeah. That was where I grew up and really what I wanted to do. Even though it was very disappointing when the factories pulled out, especially Ford. Looking back over the whole deal it was the best thing that ever happened for me. I was driving for the Wood Brothers at the time. Of course, they were the greatest people I've ever had any dealings with and still are. At the time they only ran the superspeedways and did that for years. So when Ford pulled out, I went to the Indy car circuit and ran there for a couple of years, had some good offers to run some good cars if I had

elected to stay. I knew NASCAR stock cars was where I wanted to be. So I stayed in Indy cars for a couple of years and then came back and hooked up with Junior Johnson. Now, had that problem with the factories not happened, I would have stayed with the Wood Brothers and just ran the superspeedways for years and years. But coming back and hooking up with Junior Johnson and now being the only driver to win three consecutive championships, it ended up being the best thing that ever happened to me.

Bobby Allison had just split with Junior at the end of the 1972 season and you didn't need any introduction to him.

I knew Junior, yeah. He was looking for a driver and I was looking for a ride. So we just hooked up.

Junior said he was successful because he always got drivers in their prime and by this time you were really ready to grab the world by the tail. But he was also a very talented driver and mechanic and very dedicated as a team owner, which had to help.

Junior was dedicated to that race team. Junior had never won a championship either before that. He wanted to win championships and built himself a racing team. That's exactly what I was looking for, so the chemistry was there right off the bat. You gotta work close and you gotta lay everything on the line. The first year I ran with 'em, in '73, we didn't have a whole lot of success, and we bent up some sheet metal. We ran up front almost everywhere we went, but it just seemed like everything that happened on the race track happened in front of me.

Ironically, you came up against Benny Parsons for the championship six years after you beat him for the Ford factory ride. And he won a title before you won one. Once again it came down to a make-or-break race, the season finale at Rockingham in 1973. It was decided by Benny taking advantage of the points system at the time, which included the number of miles completed. What do you remember about that day?

Benny crashed and I mean totaled his car. Of course, I thought that with a little bit of luck if I finished that race I was going to win that championship. Halfway through the race I looked up and saw a part of a car on the race track. It was Benny. They had fixed it up to where he could ride it out.

The same thing, close but no championship, happened again in 1974 versus Richard Petty.

We could have easily won it.

There was a time when the engines were not what they needed to be after the 1973 and 1974 seasons. How did you guys get through those periods in 1975 when you didn't have much confidence in the engines?

At the time, GM, I hate to say it, their equipment wasn't as good as it needed to be. That's what it amounted to when it came to (cylinder) heads and that kind of stuff. In fact, Junior and I both went to Detroit and went straight to the top and told them what we needed if we was going to stay in the racing business. We told them what they needed to do and that's what they did and that got that problem cured.

GM's participation in the mid-1970s, even though the company had officially withdrawn, was a crucial part in keeping the NASCAR Grand National division going. It didn't hurt you guys, either. They had a not-so-secret high-performance parts development program and Junior was the first in line.

Right. The back door was still open. They didn't shut both doors.

Once you guys had the reliability and engine parts you needed, you were the dominant team of the 1970s. You and Junior changed the style of racing back to the flat-out style of the factory era. The object became not only to get as many points or wins as possible, but to lead as many laps as possible and win as many poles and make sure that no one could beat you.

That was my philosophy all along. I think some of the other guys picked up on that. After they saw the way I was doing it, they knew they had to step up or not get it done. I think it made for good racing.

In 1976, you became the first driver to win four races in a row after the schedule had been shortened in 1972. The streak happened in the Fall and pretty much put the first title for you and Junior out of reach of the competition. The fourth race in that victory string was at North Wilkesboro. What was it like to win at Junior's home track in one of his cars?

That was almost as thrilling to me as winning the Daytona 500, you know. It was a great thrill to win at the tough ol' race track and in Junior's home territory. I got a lot of half-gallon jars after that. (laughter)

From time to time, I think of how many championships we would have won if I had stayed with Junior instead of deciding to start running a limited schedule in 1981. But the decision I made was right for me.

Another thing about the 1976 season; Jimmy Carter came to Darlington on Labor Day and opened the Democratic campaign at the Southern 500.

Above: *Nine seasons after winning his first in the Wood Brothers' factory Ford, Yarborough won his second Daytona 500 in 1979, driving a quasi-factory Chevy thanks to an "open back door" policy directed by Vince Piggins.*

It was special that a presidential candidate would start his campaign at one of our races. He also invited us to the White House and that was pretty special, too.

One method Junior used to resolve engine reliability problems was to perfect mid-race engine changes. In 1977, not only did you win nine races and have 25 Top-Five finishes in 30 starts, you were running at the checkered flag in every race. You guys scored 5,000 points that season in 30 races and it took 24 years and a schedule of 34 races before Jeff Gordon scored that many points in one season.

I never gave it much thought until later on and I got to thinking about it. It was amazing that somebody didn't score 5,000 again until then. What's more amazing is why somebody hasn't scored three consecutive championships again. When you think of Gordon, or Earnhardt, or Petty you would think somebody would have done it. Somebody eventually will, but it's been a long time.

You raced very well on road courses. When you began running a limited schedule in NASCAR in 1981, you got a chance to drive in the Le Mans 24-hour. What do you recall about racing Billy Hagan's Camaro on that eight-mile French circuit with all its high-speed corners and straights?

I was very impressed. It was great to add that to my resume. It was quite an honor. We ran pretty good until we had brake problems. It was a tough race track. You would go down that long back stretch and the speeds were 200 miles per hour. It was a little unusual because those French people would be sitting with their tables right beside the race track and you'd go by and there'd be whitecaps in their wine glasses. You could be going 250 miles an hour and they'd still be right there.

Another place where they love racing is Daytona. You won the Daytona 500 four times. Is there something about your style of driving that suited Daytona?

Well, I was fortunate to have won on every NASCAR track that I competed on. I liked high speed. I loved to run Daytona and loved running at North Wilkesboro, too. I loved 'em all. Daytona really kind of fit my style of driving, put it to the floor and leave it there—or try to leave it there. (Laughter.)

Daytona required a lot of knowledge when it came to chassis set-up and getting the car to go through Turn 1 and Turn 3 at the end of those long straights. Was that something you were quite good at, or learned from Junior or a little of both?
It was a little of both. And also, I studied the drafting techniques hard. I knew there had to be a whole lot to drafting. I kind of got credit for inventing the slingshot pass on the last lap. I worked hard. Earnhardt drafted good, too, even though he had a hard time winning the Daytona 500. He understood the wind and I think I understood the wind, too. I could feel the wind. The wind comes off of different cars in different ways. If you can feel it, you know where to get and when to get there. It's a talent in itself.

The question came up with Earnhardt about whether he could see the air. But really it's a question of feeling it?
Right. Feel instead of see.

I guess that's always easier with an open-face helmet, which Dale insisted on wearing. Maybe that's why he liked wearing one.
You can certainly feel much more with an open-face helmet. (Laughter.)

And you always wore an open-face helmet throughout your career.
That's right.

Darlington is another tough track. Did you have a particular knack there?
Yeah, I don't know if I wanted to do good there because I started there and it was my home race track. It was a place that I really dreaded runnin' on. I'd rather win there than anywhere else. It was such a demanding track and knowing that one mistake there would put you out. You've got to run 500 miles there and not make a single error. That's extremely hard to

Above: *Yarborough often ran competitors, and himself, ragged on short tracks. His victory at Martinsville in 1977 was one of a record eight straight on the bullrings.*

do. I know when I used to go over there and drive through the tunnel and I would get goose bumps on my arms. To this day I can drive by that place and still get those goose bumps. There's just something magic about it.

When Darrell Waltrip hit you on the back straight at Darlington and the reporters asked what happened, you said, 'Jaws! Jaws Waltrip got me.' Was that a spontaneous reaction as opposed to a nickname folks in the garage were using at the time that finally went public?
That's when the movie *Jaws* was popular. It just popped into my mind.

Another memorable day for you came at Darlington in 1985 when you were leading in the Ranier/Lundy Racing Ford. Bill Elliott was trying to win the Winston Million and was running second behind you when your power

steering went out in a plume of smoke. That had to be a pretty tough day for you.

That was the first time anybody had won the million dollars. It was a tough day, especially the last 50 laps because I had to drive that thing without power steering. If there had been ten more laps I might have caught him.

Petty, Pearson, Allison and Yarborough. During the 1970s, before regular live TV coverage, major sponsorships, and the Winston Million, you guys really kept the sport going. People often don't realize that at NASCAR's 25th anniversary in the mid-1970s the sport was in a major economic depression. Were you aware at the time you guys were racing against each other how much you were doing to sustain stock car racing?

I've always believed that those four drivers probably did more for the sport of NASCAR than anybody else in its history. Earnhardt sure did a lot, but during his era, television and all was also there. I believe we did our share of keeping it going and making it grow. We were simply just doing our job then, but some of the reporters have said that I was the original Dale Earnhardt when it came to driving just as hard as I could every lap.

Which one of you four guys—Petty, Pearson, Allison and Yarborough— do you think was the best during the 1970s?

Each of us had our good years. I won three championships and came close to some others. I think I won my share.

What about the race versus Donnie Allison at Daytona in 1979 that did so much to change NASCAR history? Before you guys crashed your cars and went to fighting in Turn 3, it appeared you got underneath him cleanly at Turn 2 and that he pulled down to block you after you were alongside.

Right. That was the slingshot. I had him beat. If I had known it was going to turn out the way it did, I'd have passed him several laps before and gone on and won the race. I wanted to do it on the last lap, which was kind of a trademark for me. I don't think he could have come back and made a pass on me, because I had already made up two laps on him.

Bobby Allison also showed up for the fight. Did you actually land any blows?

There were probably a few landed, but as soon as the firemen got in there and pulled us down, all of that kind of broke it up.

It was not that unusual to have to back up what you were doing on the track with your fists in the garage when you came along in the sport.

You had to stand your ground. You had to land a blow every once in a while. I was a minor league professional football player before I became a race car driver, but I was also a Golden Gloves boxer. I still think that fight at Daytona with Donnie was one of the best things that ever happened in NASCAR. The thing about it is, the whole Southeastern part of the United States was snowed in and Petty was half a lap down and went on and won the race and was in Victory Lane, but the cameras were down there on us. (Laughter.) They weren't even on Richard. They talk about now of penalizin' people and makin' some kind of rule about all this blocking that's goin' on at Daytona, but that was probably the original bad block.

Above: *Perhaps more amazing than winning three straight championships, Yarborough scored 5,000 points under the modern system in just 30 races in 1977.*

Cale vs Richard vs David vs Bobby

Where NASCAR roared into the consciousness of American race fans and car buffs via the factory-fueled 1960s, driver rivalries kept it afloat during the 1970s when the Detroit dollars disappeared.

You could predict Richard Petty, David Pearson, Cale Yarborough, Bobby Allison or Buddy Baker would win 70 percent of the time, but not necessarily the race-by-race results or chemistry between them. Then along came the brash and charismatic Darrell Waltrip, the only driver to break in among the established good ol' stars during the sport's economic slowdown.

The one constant was Richard Petty. "The King " won five of his championships during the 1970s. More importantly, when it got close with Yarborough in 1974 or Waltrip in 1979, he always found a way to retain the crown.

Allison was easily the most volatile, racing on four different teams after Holman-Moody shut down. Allison clearly liked beating Petty, a driver he regarded as being born with a silver accelerator under his foot. "It don't bother him getting beat unless it's me," said the King. "It's a Richard Petty complex."

But the decade will be best remembered for the rivalry between Petty and Pearson, two legends of the 1960s who helped sustain the old Chrysler vs Ford battles with Dodge vs Mercury. Their fights for supremacy culminated in what many regard as the greatest race in NASCAR history, the 1976 Daytona 500. Petty failed to close the door on Pearson as they approached the checkers, hitting his adversary. Pearson hit the wall, then Petty, as both crashed. The crippled Wood Brothers Mercury crawled across the line ahead of the Petty Enterprises Dodge. Yet the most decisive Grand National race happened three years later in Daytona when Yarborough, who had stamped his own signature on the history books with three straight dominating title seasons, was crashed by Donnie Allison on the last lap as they contested the lead. Next, Cale fought Donnie and brother Bobby with his fist and helmet during a live CBS Sports broadcast that scored excellent ratings and heralded the electronic wealth of the 1980s.

Cale vs Richard vs David vs Bobby

Above: Bobby Allison, here driving a Junior Johnson Chevy, finished one-two with Richard Petty 20 times during the 1971–72 seasons. A perfect day, said Allison, was "knowing my car was the best that day and Richard Petty was really upset."

Left: A handful of star drivers and teams dominated after the factory pullouts. But the independents still had their moments. James Hylton won at Talladega in 1972, one of two career victories. The draft was the great equalizer on the gigantic 2.66-mile oval and 12 different drivers won the Alabama track's first 12 summertime events before Darrell Waltrip repeated in 1982.

Right: After prevailing in the constant arguments with factories, building two major speedways at Daytona and Talladega, and establishing NASCAR as the premier stock car circuit. William Henry Getty "Big Bill" France, age 62, turned over the presidency to son William Clifton France in 1972.

Previous page: With sponsorship increasingly important, so were "photo opportunities." Matador driver Bobby Allison poses with Bebop Hobel, Miss Winston, in 1974 at Pocono, Pa.

Right *Losing his drivers to other racing series was always a concern for "Big Bill" France, especially when "his" stars Bobby and Donnie Allison, Cale Yarborough and Lee Roy Yarbrough began competing in the Indy 500 after the withdrawal of the factories from NASCAR in the early 1970s. But often enough, it worked the other way as Indy 500 winners A.J. Foyt (seen getting the 1971 pole award in Atlanta from then Governor Jimmy Carter (on pages 68–69), Mark Donohue and Parnelli Jones crossed over to NASCAR and won races in the 1970s. Occasionally, Europeans would show up. Former F-1 and sports car driver Jackie Oliver, seen in the garage leaning against Junie Donlavey's Ford, however, was not a threat to win.*

Below: *Bobby Isaac left the potent Harry Hyde-built Dodge Chargers of Nord Kauskropf (owner of K&K Insurance) at the end of the 1972 season when all the victories disappeared. Buddy Baker switched from Petty Engineering and soon won at Texas Motor Speedway. The victories never came back for Issac. In 1973, Isaac said a voice had told him to "Get out of the car" while on the back straight at Talladega in a Bud Moore Ford. He promptly parked the car and lost his ride. Ironically, Isaac received a gold watch from Bill France as the only regular to compete at Talladega in 1969 when the Grand National drivers went on strike due to concerns about high speeds. Due to those speeds, by 1972 the Dodges like this one had restrictor plates on their big block engines, paving the way for the switch to small blocks, completed by 1974.*

Cale vs Richard vs David vs Bobby

Above: *Big Buddy Baker scored 19 career wins and 40 poles, but fell short of the records of the Big Four —Petty, Pearson, Yarborough and Allison. Harry Hyde, to Baker's right, won 56 races and 88 poles as a crew chief.*

Left: *Dick Brooks' haggard eyes show the strain of winning in 1973 at Talladega, where the little known Crawford brothers of Fayetteville, Ga. defeated the restrictor plates with a clever manifold design, outlawed immediately afterward by NASCAR.*

Right: *Bobby Allison drove for three different teams in 1971–73. But he kept winning on short tracks, superspeedways and the road courses. In 1973 he drove his own Chevy to one of his league-leading six career victories at Riverside, Calif.'s road circuit.*

Right: A year after winning the Indy 500 in 1972 for team owner Roger Penske, Mark Donohue drove to his only career Grand National victory in Penske's Matador at Riverside, Calif.'s road course.

An incomparable Can-Am and Indy car driver, Donohue then set a closed course speed record of 221 mph at Talladega. Donohue retired temporarily and Penske hired Bobby Allison, who won four more races for "The Captain" in 1974–75. After Allison's victory in the Matador at the Ontario Motor Speedway, Penske garnered the largest fine in NASCAR history at the time ($9,100) for illegal roller tappets in the engine.

By that time, the future was clear for NASCAR technically. The absence of the factories brought the benefit of standardization of equipment, which in turn made rule-making easier. The only eligible engines became the 358 cubic inch version of the V-8 small block readily available to both GM and Ford teams. The 115-inch wheelbase tube frame cars, meanwhile, had to have two-door stock bodywork that could fit templates. The body designs were supposed to be no older than three years, a rule extended to four in 1978 to give "The King" another year in the Dodge Charger

Penske left the Winston Cup in 1977 after failing to get American Motors committed to NASCAR. He went on to 11 victories in the Indy 500 by the year 2001 and a squeaky clean reputation despite earlier cheating scandals in both NASCAR and sports car road racing. Penske also founded Championship Auto Racing Teams, which sanctioned Indy cars, as well as operating race tracks in Brooklyn, Mich., Rockingham, N.C., Nazareth, Pa., Homestead, Fla. and Fontana, Calif. Penske returned to NASCAR in 1990, and in 2000 sold his tracks to the France family, becoming the International Speedway Corporation's second largest shareholder.

Above: *Petty and Yarborough were side-by-side with ten wins in 1974, but on this day at Michigan International Speedway it was David Pearson, winner of 11 races the year before, who took top honors.*

Right: *Canadian Earl Ross, a rookie who won at Martinsville in 1974, became the only foreign-born driver to win in the first five decades of NASCAR's premier series. Petty, Yarborough, Allison and Pearson won all the other races that year.*

Above and below: Benny Parsons and his L.G. DeWitt team celebrate victory in the Daytona 500. Below, they celebrate his championship two years earlier in 1973. Note the lack of bodywork on Parsons' car, re-built after a crash to get enough miles for the title. The formula for points was changed two years later to exclude any mileage considerations.

Left: Darrell Waltrip became the most influential driver of the late 1970s and early 1980s by driving and talking a good game. He castigated the star system that had grown up around Petty, Pearson, Yarborough, and Allison, using the media to force NASCAR to reduce favoritism.

Above: *Yarborough drove hard and laughed heartedly quite often. "Silver Fox" David Pearson started from the pole at the Darlington track in 1973 where he won a record ten times and got his nickname.*

Right: *Pearson celebrates Daytona 500 after chugging across the finish line at 20 mph in his crippled car. When the crash started with Petty, Pearson radioed Crew Chief Leonard Wood: "The (****) hit me."*

Bottom right: *Ricky Rudd, who would eventually set the record for consecutive starts, began at the age of 19 and drove four seasons for his father before landing a regular ride with DiGard, replacing Darrell Waltrip.*

Right: The France family and the French who ran the Le Mans 24-hour had much in common in the 1970s. Daytona hosted the world's other most prominent 24-hour race for sports cars starting in 1966 under sanction from the International Motor Sports Association, co-founded and owned by the France family. During the 1970s, Le Mans and the Daytona owners also had a common enemy in open-wheel racing. For the LeMans officials, Formula 1 was the big headache and for the France family Indy cars remained an obstacle to dominance due to the majestic standing of the Indy 500.

The Frances and Le Mans officials worked hard at co-operating for their common good, especially when it came to improving their respective 24-hour races. So it wasn't a surprise that Camaro entries from Herschel McGriff and Doug McGriff plus Dick Hutcherson and Dick Brooks competed at Le Mans in 1976, where the French fans loved the earthy roar of the American V-8's.

"Big Bill" France wasn't just worried about Indy cars when it came to open-wheel racing. The presence of the first U.S. Grand Prix for Formula 1 cars in nearby Sebring, Fla. in 1959, the same year he opened the Daytona International Speedway, gave him great concern. But the U.S. Grand Prix race moved to Riverside, Calif. and then on to Watkins Glen, N.Y.

France considered running a series for Indy-type cars and had an experimental one built. Daytona's own Marshall Teague died while testing it at the Florida track, scuttling any plans. Daytona's high banks were designed for full-bodied cars and the Frances then concentrated on improving stock car racing's appeal. Ironically, the first real race car of "Big Bill" was a canvas-bodied open-wheel machine based on a Model T drive train he built while running a gas station in Washington, D.C. as a young man.

Left: *Yarborough and Johnson celebrate victory at Daytona in 1977. It would be a different story two years later in a fateful finish. Crew Chief Herb Nab is to Yarborough's right.*

Below: *Janet Guthrie became the first female to race in both the Indy 500 and the Daytona 500 in 1977. Guthrie liked to say that: "You don't carry the car on your shoulder, you drive it," when talking about her efforts to win a race. A physicist, pilot, astronaut candidate and sports car driver, Guthrie suffered various forms of chauvinism.*

Guthrie finished sixth at Bristol in 1977, her best result on a track considered the most physically demanding on the circuit.

Above: Neil Bonnett, a second generation member of the Alabama Gang, scores his first win for car owner Jim Stacy in 1977 at Ontario, California.

Right: Wearing the trademark lightning bolt of Gatorade, Darrell Waltrip steps into the Chevy owned by Hoss Ellington at Talladega in 1977. The regular driver of the Hawaiian Tropic-sponsored entry, original Alabama Gang member Donnie Allison, got sick and needed relief. Since NASCAR credited the starting driver for any result, Allison got the victory and thus the streak of different winners at Talladega's summer race was sustained.

Left: *Yarborough, an excellent road racer, started his campaign for a hat–trick of championships with a victory at Riverside, Calif.*

Right: *Bobby Allison dodged a pothole in an ill-handling Ford with bent fenders to win the Daytona 500 in 1978 for car owner Bud Moore, whose first victory as an entrant came with Joe Weatherly in 1962. It was Moore's only victory in NASCAR's biggest race and a very happy Allison's first after 15 starts. He would win two more in the next nine attempts.*

Below: *Little Lennie Pond won his only race in 1978 at Talladega before walking away from racing not long afterward. Pond beat runner-up Bobby Allison by an inch or two, as demonstrated by the owner of his Olds, Harry Ranier.*

Cale vs Richard vs David vs Bobby

Left: Dale Earnhardt and Crew Chief Jake Elder celebrate the second-generation driver's first victory at Bristol in 1979.

Top right: Yarborough, who had little love lost for Bobby Allison, flails at him with his helmet as the Alabama Gang member comes to the aid of brother Donnie following the last lap of the 1979 Daytona 500. The duel for victory between Cale and Donnie ended in grief at the Turn 3 wall and the world watched the fight unfold on CBS Sports' first live telecast of the race.

Below: Richard Petty and crew, half a lap behind at the start of the final circuit, head for Victory Lane after the crash of Allison and Yarborough.

Bottom right: The end of an era. The wheels fall off the Wood Brothers Mercury of David Pearson at the end of pit road at Darlington after a miscommunication during a pit stop. Pearson was fired a few days later.

Bill Elliott

Bill Elliott and his community-run team, including brothers Ernie and Dan plus father George, re-wrote the NASCAR history book in 1985. Awesome Bill and his fellow heroes from a little town in north Georgia had a stunning season, coming away with a record 11 superspeedway victories, 11 poles and the first Winston Million title. The sudden explosion in media coverage for NASCAR was unprecedented and would not be equalled for another 16 years, when Dale Earnhardt suffered his fatal accident in Daytona.

Your father George often remarked how hard you and your brothers worked when you first started racing in the Winston Cup Series. But you also had a lot of help from people in Dawson County, back when you guys had your garage in the old schoolhouse that your father had converted into a Ford dealership. What kind of support did you have?
We had several people who would work their jobs all day long and come in after work and contribute whatever they could do. You had several of those guys you could depend on to do whatever you needed done. Those were the people who along the way were forgotten, even doing small jobs.

That was the old-fashioned way of racing, wasn't it?
We didn't pay very well, but we fed them good. There's other ways to compensate people for their effort and time. We were grateful for everything they did. There were a lot of people who believed in me throughout the years and gave their support.

One guy from Michigan who was really important to your career was Harry Melling. Harry bought the team from your father and gave you the financing to keep going in 1982. Things might have turned out differently had that not happened, but you guys seemed determined to continue one way or another.

There's a lot of what ifs in life. We worked awful hard at what we knew. I think we were able to find the right door to open to get to the next step. My life has been a strange deal over the years. I've made some bad decisions in some areas, but they've all led to a better deal. Just like when my Dad started, he couldn't afford to do it, but it led to a better deal. Jim Knutson up in Michigan also helped us a lot. Our friendship with him is what got Harry Melling into racing. Then Benny came back and said to Harry, 'Look, help these guys out.' A lot of the groundwork had already been laid. It was because our performance kept stepping up. They saw an opportunity. Look, here's a kid and you're talking a minimal amount of money. Take a chance. Two thousand dollars a race for 12 races back in '81, yes it was a lot of money. In the whole scheme of things, look at what millions today people spend on these cars taking a chance to see if a team is going to work or not.

In 1982, Harry bought the team from your father right after the Atlanta race and the team began running the full schedule the following year with Coors sponsorship. There was another big development in 1983, also, because that was the first year of the re-modeled Ford Thunderbird. That was good timing, but it took a while to develop the car. How much did you work on the car?

Above: *Cigar-chomping Harry Melling bought the family-run outfit from George Elliott in 1982, but it took six years and a gutsy comeback from the overwhelming year of 1985 to build a Winston Cup championship team.*

Bill Elliott

104

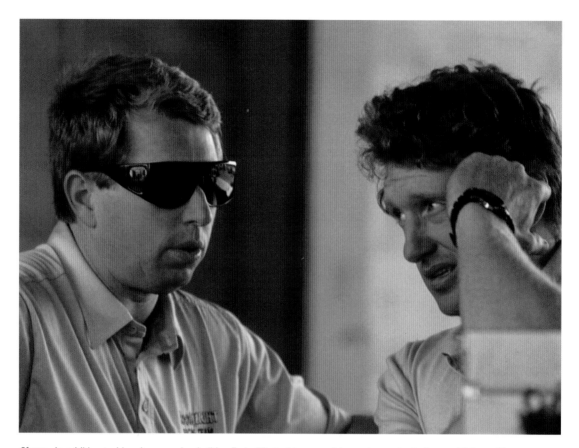

Above: *In addition to his role as engine builder, Ernie Elliott did many of the tasks required of crew chiefs, making set-up decisions with his younger brother and calling race strategy from the pit wall.*

I did everything. We were so limited on resources. You know you might get a wind tunnel day every so often, because you were just in the line of the Ford deal. As our performance continued to build, we got more and more time. Still, back then in '85 there was 11 of us in the shop counting me. That included the motor side with Ernie and chassis side. Shoot, it was killin' us. That's where I started having a hard time dealing with any of this stuff because I resented anything that took me away from the race car. If the race car performed then everything took care of itself. It's always the same. If you ain't runnin' good, then you have to find somebody to talk to. If you're runnin' good, then that becomes a moot point. They've got to write about you, good, bad or indifferent. Still those days…there was so much changin' going on back then. NASCAR was continuing to build their deal, television was getting more and more involved. We were crossin' a lot of

different roads, going a lot of different directions. I don't see how we did it with the amount of people we had. There was a lot of sacrifice from a lot of us just to get where we were at.

Ernie worked an incredible number of hours. Evidently, he gradually increased the RPM and power without losing reliability from the Windsor block of Ford.
He had good reliable stuff. I still say that when Ernie's on his game there ain't nobody any better in the motor department as far as understanding cylinder heads and intake manifolds and the works of an engine. Shoot, he's done it ever since he was a kid. I'd put him up against the best of them.

And he was self-taught and had never worked for another team in the Winston Cup.
Exactly. The biggest thing we had going for us was we

were down there in Dawsonville and nobody knew what the heck we were doin'. We were in our own little world.

You guys changed the way people ran on the big tracks. Prior to the 1985 season, teams used to run narrow cars at Daytona to increase speeds on the straights and then hope the driver could hold on in the corners. You guys turned that formula around with the Thunderbird to where getting in the corners and sustaining the speed through the middle and off the corners was as important. We didn't even think about it. We just worked in every area we possibly could to make the car better, aero-wise, handling-wise. I never tried to concentrate on one deal, just like these guys today. Where we took racing to the next level then, all these race engineers are taking it to the next level now.

What do you remember about winning your first Daytona 500 in 1985?
I remember everything. I can remember running the 125s and running the race on Sunday and running against Cale most of the day. Cale had a good car and had some problems, but he would have been tough. It was like something that just happened and it was gone, then you were ready for the next race. If you can learn to ride the rollercoaster, some days you're up and some days you're down, just go on and forget about it. If the highs don't get too high and the lows don't get too low, you can get on an even scale and live with it. All through the times that are bad, there'll be this other guy that comes along and then another guy. That's the way it is.

You actually broke your leg when your Thunderbird tagged the wall at Rockingham at the next superspeedway race that year. You had a hairline fracture, but continued what became your "Awesome" season by winning in Atlanta. How badly were you hurting in Atlanta from that broken leg?
Not too bad. It wasn't no big deal. I just had a hard time getting around. I can remember coming in on crutches trying to work on the race car (laughter). My leg felt like a watermelon, because I stayed on it so much and it was swollen so much. At that time, you just did whatever you had to do.

Above: *Rule changes in 1985, designed to slow Elliott's T-Bird, brought death threat letters to the France family from an irate, anonymous Ford fan.*

At Talladega that year, early in the race you had a problem with an oil line and pitted. The team fixed the oil line and also had what amounted to a slightly out-of-sequence pit stop. You might have been two laps down on the scoreboard at the time, but when Cale and the rest of the leaders came in for their regular stops and everybody was back on the same schedule, you weren't two laps down.
It was one-and-three-quarters of a lap.

Still, it is pretty remarkable to gain that much ground on the track under green and to still come on to win the race.
A lot of those guys beat themselves. That day I had my car where I could run it wide open. It didn't seem like Cale could. A lot of cars fell out that day, blew up and couldn't run the pace. There again Ernie's stuff held up and ran all day.

That put you in position to win the Winston Million. When they announced it the previous year in New York City during the Winston Cup banquet, did you think at that time you would be in a position to win it?

I was sittin' there at that table and sayin', 'Man, that's a big deal. It would be nice to win. But I've never won Daytona, I've never won a lot of races they're talkin' about.' It's one of those deals that passes through your mind, but on the second thought it's the farthest thing from it.

You ran your race to win at Darlington in the Southern 500 to clinch the Winston Million. The race came to you. Dale Earnhardt was running second late in the race and he put his nose into the wall at Turn 2 and drifted back down the track. You were running third and nearly hit him. That looked like the closest call of the day.

A lot of luck had to come my way. There were several bullets I dodged. Cale's power steering broke right in front of me while he was leading. It was like one of them deals that just unfolded. We played our game. We did what we needed to do.

There were a lot of rules changes for the Fords that year, including ride height, a carburetion change and a change in the height of the roofline of the Thunderbird. How discouraged were you and the team by NASCAR's response to your dominance?

I think we were pretty upset. But what do you do? We worked so hard to get an advantage and it was so easy to be taken away. The problem we had was that we didn't have enough people to respond to the changes. That's what hurt us the next year, with burn-out and Ernie being sick. That's what really hurt us in the '86 season.

A lot of people in 1985 had the perception that what hurt you in the championship at the end of the year was the short tracks. Actually, you had a pretty good short track program, but what really hurt you were the races on the same superspeedways you had done well on earlier in the year.

At Martinsville I was running fifth and they had a big pile-up. We had a problem with some parts. The flywheel bolts broke at Bristol and North Wilkesboro. That's what the problem was.

It seemed poetic that you won the race in Atlanta near the end of the season to clinch your record 11th victory at the same track where you once came and watched David Pearson, who held the record for superspeedway victories in one season up until that time.

One of these days after I stop racin', I'll sit back and think about all those weird things that happened.

What was it like coming to the Atlanta track where you used to watch the races when you were younger?

I came here and sat in the infield and that's when Pearson won the spring race.

Pearson was very smooth and consistent, the same style you have. How much did your admiration for Pearson's driving influence your own driving style?

That's just the way I grew up. I worked on my own cars. I never tried to tear it up. If I tore the fender off, I was the one who had to go back and put it on again. If I couldn't beat a guy, then I went back and worked harder on my stuff and figured out how to beat him. Racing's changed and that's why I struggle at some of these places. The tactics that are used in racin', maybe that is racin'. But it's still hard to deal with.

It still seems to work for you as far as the end of the year when it comes to the points.

Everybody's got their own style. It's worked for me and I don't see any need to change it.

In '87 when you won your second Daytona 500 from the pole, one moment stands out where Dale Earnhardt went door-to-door with you coming off Turn 4 and actually hit your car. That was about the time when he was really changing the rules of the road and using his fenders on all the speedways and superspeedways as well as the short tracks.

He tried to shake you up and intimidate you, whatever he tried to do. The main thing about that race...it came down to a late splash of gas and quickie deal and a run to the end. It was close.

Ironically, it was Benny Parsons who was second. That same year, the so-called "Pass in the Grass" took place in Charlotte. You were leading the field coming to the flag stand for the re-start of the final ten laps under green.

Above: *Elliott beat buddy Benny Parsons and the rain to score his first career win at Riverside in 1983. Winston's Jerry Long, to the right of Elliott's first wife Martha, would hand over $1 million at Darlington in 1985.*

Earnhardt tagged Bodine in the first turn and then all hell broke loose. On the next re-start, Dale was leading and you were behind him. It seemed that Dale came down on you. You had the run on him and he came down on you, turned himself, got into the grass and then came back out onto the track. But he never lost the lead.

That was a very weird day. The way the tri-oval is at Charlotte, I had my nose stuck there and Earnhardt turned for the tri-oval instead of giving me enough room. He was either going to run me in the grass or make me spin him out. But it wouldn't have been my fault. He turned for the tri-oval and he run in the grass, I backed off and he still had the position. It all came back to the start (before that). The caution car never got out of the way, Geoff Bodine started (from the outside front row) and they never called off the start. We go down into the corner and everybody gets together, everybody gets spun out and it's all over but the crying.

It must have been satisfying for you guys to figure out what you needed to come back and win the championship in 1988 after Earnhardt and the Childress team had won the title in 1986–87.

It was. I still look back on those days and the biggest, proudest thing for me is that we did it our way. It was all of us down there in Dawsonville. We didn't buy into the deal, we put it all together. Somebody made the comment the other day when I was coming into a track on race day that he'd never seen a driver up so early. I told him, 'You didn't see me back in the '80s. Sometimes they let you in the garage at 5 a.m. and I was right there at 5 a.m.'

You have no regrets about taking it easy in the season finale in Atlanta to make sure you beat Rusty Wallace to the championship?

God no. Rusty criticized me so bad and he did the same thing next year. You gotta do what you gotta do.

The Big E's

Dale Earnhardt started his roll to seven championships in 1980, the first young upstart to officially upset the star system of the 1970s. Another Big E, Bill Elliott won a record 11 superspeedway victories and the first Winston Million in 1985. Reporters rallied from all over the country to report on "Awesome Bill from Dawsonville."

Along with Darrell Waltrip, the first to challenge the older stars, Earnhardt and Elliott established a new order. But it wouldn't have happened without a new cast of team owners. By the 1980s businessmen saw attractive opportunities in the ownership of a Winston Cup racing team.

Bill Gardner's DiGard Racing had launched Waltrip. California businessman Rod Osterlund then funded Earnhardt's entry into the big leagues and his first championship. Michigan industrialist Harry Melling saved the Elliott family team from a financial downfall. Some of the big spenders ran out of cash and disappeared such as Warner Hodgdon and Jim Stacy. Some eventually lost interest after winning their share like M.C. Anderson and Harry Ranier. Others like Rick

Hendrick, Jack Roush and Felix Sabates became the prototypes for Winston Cup success by investing heavily. Engine builder Robert Yates and driver Richard Childress became team owners due to sponsorship, factory backing and the rising purses.

Ultimately, corporate sponsorship meant upward mobility for all. R.J. Reynolds Tobacco Co. became a market leader with the Winston Million, The Winston all-star race and its title sponsorship (NASCAR switched the Grand National name to the Busch Series). GM and Ford, which revived Special Vehicle Operations, began once again to sell brand loyalty and performance parts through stock car racing. The emergence of cable television and live race coverage fueled the desire for airtime by all sponsors.

Above: *Richard Petty broke his neck in a crash at Pocono in the summer of 1980. But he started the next race at Talladega before giving way to relief driver Joe Millikan. NASCAR was aware of the injury but allowed "The King" to race nevertheless.*

The Big E's

Above: *Richard Petty broke his neck in an accident when his Chevy cut a tire at Pocono, Pa. midway in the 1980 season. He showed up at Talladega a week later with a neck brace (opposite) and his helmet. Petty started his Chevy (above) and handed over to relief driver Joe Millikan after one lap. Two weeks later, Petty drove the entire race at Michigan, not easy given that drivers had to manhandle the 115-inch wheelbase monsters, which were in their last season. The injury knocked "The King" out of first place in the points, leaving the battle to Cale Yarborough and Dale Earnhardt.*

Left: *The news is out. Earnhardt beat three-time champion Yarborough to the Winston Cup in the 1980 season finale at Ontario, Calif. in a major upset—despite running over his jack in the pits. Earnhardt sustained the Rod Osterlund team with aggressive tactics even though Yarborough won the previous two races at Rockingham, N.C. and Atlanta.*

Above: *Despite the attempts to sabotage his gas tank with sugar, Bobby Allison toasts his 1983 Winston Cup victory at Riverside with (from left) car owner Bill Gardner, engine man Robert Yates and crew chief Gary Nelson.*

Opposite top: *Dale Earnhardt won three races in the Fords of Bud Moore in the 1982–83 seasons before switching to Richard Childress Racing.*

Opposite bottom: *DW and Junior celebrate with Flossie Johnson and Warner Hodgdon's wife Sharon. Hodgdon was one of several money men who left abruptly in the early 1980s.*

Above: Dave Marcis (71) won this 1982 Richmond, Va. race because he didn't damage his car in the collision with Joe Millikan and he was in front when the rain fell.

Left: Tim Richmond arrived with a winning pedigree: Rookie of the Year honors at the 1980 Indianapolis 500. He won his first Winston Cup race in 1982 at Riverside aboard J.D. Stacy's Buick in his 44th start.

Above: Maurice Petty secretly built brother Richard an oversize V-8 in 1983 to protest cheating by others. NASCAR's new procedures ended engine scandals.

Above: If the rain had fallen a few minutes earlier at Riverside in 1983, Bill Elliott's first Winston Cup win would have been postponed in favor of Benny Parsons.

The Big E's

Above: Firsts fell more often than rain in the California desert at Riverside. Car owner Richard Childress and driver Ricky Rudd got their first win there together in 1983. Crew chief Kirk Shelmerdine, to the left, hoists Childress.

Main picture: The speed secret to the 110-inch wheelbase cars at Daytona initially concerned taking advantage of the cars' smaller size. With no minimum front track width rules, teams tended to narrow up the already smaller cars for less drag on the straight—and hope the driver could hold on in the corners.

Waddell Wilson's Pontiac produced the best top-end horsepower at the time and Cale Yarborough wasn't bashful about holding the pedal down. He ran the first official lap over 200 mph in 1982 in qualifying for the Daytona 500. But on his second lap, the intrepid driver lost control in Turn 2, wrecking his Pontiac Le Mans.

Since the rules required any driver replacing his car to give up his qualifying time, Yarborough's lap of 200.503 mph seemingly went for naught. But with his back-up machine, Yarborough earned an eighth place starting position in his Twin 125-mile qualifying race. In the feature, he used a last-lap slingshot maneuver to pass Buddy Baker to claim his third Daytona 500 victory.

Within three years, the Elliott brothers began taking advantage of both the relatively small size of the 1983 Thunderbird and its aerodynamic shape. With Bill Elliott's awesome year in 1985, starting with a Daytona 500 victory from the pole, they radically improved the equation. Top-end speed was enhanced by consistent cornering and getting a good exit onto the straights. Their methods also proved less hazardous to the driver and the car.

The Big E's

Above: Dan, Bill and Ernie Elliott celebrate their victory at Rockingham, N.C., which kept them in the title hunt for the Winston Cup. Contenders Harry Gant and Terry Labonte finished second and third respectively.

Right: Elliott wins the first of two Daytona 500 victories in the Coors Ford of Melling Racing.

Opposite page: Petty said his 200th win against Yarborough in July of 1984 at Daytona came from successfully completing the move that failed versus David Pearson in 1976. Rumors persisted that he had an oversize engine as well. It was his last victory.

The Big E's

Top: *Million Dollar Bill brought unprecedented coverage to NASCAR's Winston Cup when Earnhardt crashed and the power steering failed on Yarborough's Ford, opening up Darlington's Victory Lane.*

Above: *Tim Richmond dashed to a streak of six wins and two seconds in ten starts during his incomparable seven-win 1986 season, including the victory in NASCAR's return to the Watkins Glen, N.Y.'s road circuit.*

Opposite page: *Darrell Waltrip led the league in victories five times in the six seasons from 1979–84. His triumph at Michigan with crew chief Jeff Hammond (at right) in 1984 was one of seven.*

Left: *Improved consistency and five wins brought Dale Earnhardt and Richard Childress the first of their six championships together in 1986. The trophy is shared here with their wives, Judy, left, and Teresa.*

Below: *Tim Richmond, knowing that he was dying of AIDS, scored the penultimate victory of his career at Pocono, Pa. in 1987. After a win the following week at Riverside, his erratic driving and concerns about drug use forced him out of the Hendrick Motorsports Chevy.*

Opposite page: *A quiet moment for the shy kid from Dawsonville, Ga., who took to fame like a duck to motor oil.*

Above: *Davey Allison visits Victory Lane after father Bobby beat him by a car length to win his third Daytona 500. Within five months Allison would nearly lose his life and within five years he would lose both Davey and son Clifford.*

Right: *Easy-going Neil Bonnett surprised people not only with a victory for the Rahmoc team at Richmond in 1988, he gave Hoosier Tires its first victory in the upstart Indiana company's second Winston Cup race.*

Right: *Bill Elliott tiptoed to 11th place at his home track in Atlanta to claim the Winston Cup by 24 points over Rusty Wallace, who led the most laps and won.*

Below: *Alan Kulwicki became the fourth driver to win his first race in 1989, but was first to run a "Polish victory lap" afterward. He took a wrong way tour of the Phoenix track, saying the fans could see him better that way.*

Above: *The June 1988 crash at Pocono raceway after a cut tire nearly claimed the life of Bobby Allison and forced him to retire.*

Below: *After six wins, Rusty Wallace beat both Mark Martin and Dale Earnhardt to the Winston Cup at the 1989 season finale in Atlanta.*

Opposite page: *Always appreciative of the sponsorship of R.J. Reynolds Tobacco Co., Dick Trickle was 48 when he won the Winston Cup rookie title.*

Top: *Terry Labonte scored four wins in three seasons with Junior Johnson. The "Iceman" unleashes the champagne at Pocono in 1989.*

Above: *Team owner Junie Donlavey and driver Jody Ridley scored their only Winston Cup victory at Dover, Del in 1981.*

Left: *Ernie Irvan hit pay dirt in 1990 at Bristol, Tenn.,three races after he was hired to drive the Chevy of Morgan-McClure. The next year he won the Daytona 500.*

Above: Leader Brett Bodine, driving Kenny Bernstein's Buick, passes Davey Allison (28) at North Wilkesboro, N.C. When NASCAR picked up the second-placed car during a caution, Bodine got an extra pit stop without losing the lead and scored his only career victory, directed by Larry McReynolds.

Left: The Miracle on Volusia Boulevard. Derrike Cope won the 1990 Daytona 500 when leader Dale Earnhardt cut a tire in Turn 3 on the last lap. Cope's crew chief, Buddy Parrott, elected to take only two tires on the final pit stop, putting him second until fate intervened.

Above: Mark Martin drove for seven different team owners, including himself, before finding the right match with Ford team owner Jack Roush in 1988. They won their first Winston Cup race a year later at Rockingham, N.C.

Above: *Dale Jarrett was never slow, but took some time to get to the Winston Cup, starting at age 31. He won his first race at Michigan at age 34 for the Wood Brothers in 1991 as father Ned Jarrett made the call on TV for CBS Sports.*

Jeff Gordon

Three decades after Fred Lorenzen, Jeff Gordon was the second ultra-talented Golden Boy to arrive in the Winston Cup. Fully prepared by racing from the age of five, Gordon started in a plum ride with Hendrick Motorsports at age 21 in 1992. Where Lorenzen's mentor was Ralph Moody, Gordon had Ray Evernham. Unlike Lorenzen, Gordon stepped into a NASCAR series that was relatively safe, stable and popular.

Your fourth title in 2002 moved you past three-time winners Lee Petty, David Pearson, Cale Yarborough and Darrell Waltrip. Only Richard Petty and Dale Earnhardt recorded more than three championships, which puts you in some pretty unique company.

I don't know how those last two guys won so many championships. There's just so much that goes into being champion. It just takes so much out of you. I look at who's won three (titles), who had two, who's had one, and then Petty and Earnhardt, who had seven. It's an unbelievable league of company to be with.

You won four titles at Hendrick Motorsports by the age of 30. That makes you an odds-on favorite to pass Petty and Earnhardt by winning eight championships.

We just think about the next one and try not to get too far ahead of ourselves.

There's a lot of people who compare you to Michael Jordan in the way that you have dominated Winston Cup racing just like he has dominated the NBA. Do you see yourself as a great athlete like Jordan?

I'm not one to go out and say I'm the greatest and that I want to be the best. I want to have respect and I want people to think I have talent. I look at motor racing as unique to any other sport out there. A baseball pitcher can control his own destiny because the ball is in his hands. In motor racing, there's a lot riding on the car and the team. When it comes to

basketball, no doubt about it Michael Jordan is the best—an awesome basketball player. He's the best in the NBA. But if you ask him whether he'd rather be a great player or winning, I guarantee you he'd rather be winning. In my case, I just want to be a part of the greatest team.

Your first Winston Cup start came in Richard Petty's last race. But you raced regularly against Dale Earnhardt and clinched your first championship with him right on your heels in 1995. What did you learn from him about how to win championships?

I learned a lot from him on the track racing side-by-side. Even though I watched him race for championships before, I got to see first-hand what it was like battling with him for a title in 1995. He was just so good at knowing when to win and when to bring it home for the points. Some guys have a special knack for knowing how to get the most they can out of the car every time they're out there on the racetrack. He looked at the big picture and he knew he wanted to be an eight-time champion. He had seven of them because he knew what he was doing. I don't know how the heck our team won that championship in '95. He knew where he could shine and he knew where he just had to get all that he could out of the race. He never gave up. I learned a lot from him. Winning races is great, but there's nothing quite like winning championships.

Above: *His stepfather moved Gordon from California to Indiana so the teenager could hone his racing skills in sprint cars. When Indy car teams yawned, Gordon headed for NASCAR.*

Jeff Gordon

Both Earnhardt and Petty set a standard for how to handle the role of great champions. Was that something else you learned from Earnhardt?

I realized after winning my first championship that there are responsibilities and expectations that come along with that. Whether you want them or not, they're there. I love being a champion and so I've learned how to enjoy the responsibilities that come along with it. I want to be a good champion and represent the sport the best way I know how. And I'm comfortable with that. If I wasn't, I'd retire now.

How did you cope after Earnhardt's fatal crash in the Daytona 500?

I had so much respect for him on and off the track. There were times when I dreaded seeing that black No. 3 in my mirror and there were times that I didn't. If you were racing him, you knew you were racing the best there was. If you beat him, you knew you accomplished something far greater than you could ever imagine. If you got beat by him, you knew you got beat by the best. I'll never forget the memories I have of Dale and I credit him for bringing me to a new level. His crash created a huge loss. Like any time you have a loss, whether it's in sport or in the family or anybody close, you step back and look at life and put things into perspective and what your priorities are. You go home and be thankful for the things that mean the most to you. I was thankful for a lot of things and counted my blessings and said I would work as hard as I can and be the best race car driver I can be and the best person I can be.

As the man everybody guns for in the Winston Cup, do you find that an enjoyable role?

I don't know anybody that doesn't like being on top of their sport as often as possible. Sure, there's responsibilities that come along with that and pressures. But those pressures and responsibilities are a whole lot better than sitting back there tenth in points. I'm very passionate about the sport. I really have enjoyed seeing it grow, motorsports in general but especially NASCAR. I've gotten a lot of joy out of playing my role and being a small part of that. I hope to continue to see it grow and play whatever role I can to help it get to the level it deserves to be.

Does being the kingpin have its advantages?

When you've gone through championship seasons and quite a few races, it allows you to have that confidence that no matter what situation you're dealt with you can get through it. The 2000 season taught me more than anything in racing. We got knocked down a few notches after Ray Evernham left as the crew chief and we had to claw our way back to the top and work harder. We had the resources and we had great people and we just had to get that chemistry. Once it started to form and everything else started to fall along with it. As long as we stay focused on what we're doing and don't beat ourselves, I think we can win many more races and championships. I don't look out there and think who's the guy to beat? I think in terms of whether we're beating ourselves.

Your first three titles came with Evernham as the crew chief and he was given a lot of credit for your success. It says a lot that you were able to keep winning races and championships at Hendrick Motorsports after he left and offered to take you with him as a part owner of his new Dodge team. Did you become more of a team leader after he left?

When Ray left there was a void. He was an outspoken leader and we knew we needed to re-structure the team, starting with putting Brian Whitesell in charge as the team manager and then bringing Robbie Loomis on as the crew chief. I don't feel like I became the team leader. But I did step up and I led the team meetings on race day. I don't get to the shops as much as I would like to, but the guys do look at me differently. We also became one of the first teams to have someone other than the crew chief operating as the team manager. Brian is also an engineer in addition to the team manager. Other teams started following that. It got so that the crew chief can't do it all. We're going to start having more engineers and more computers and more (computer) simulations. That's the way it's going to go.

But the sport still depends on the guy who sits behind the wheel, not only from the driving side but also from the point of view of his knowledge of how the car works. Have you improved over the years when it comes to knowledge of the chassis?

You've got to be able to communicate with the crew chief. When Robbie and I first started out, Robbie was nervous on the radio. He's come a long way since then and I've always said he has the whole package. The way Robbie and I started out in our relationship, I was a lot more interested in what the car felt like going into the corner than what was under it. My part is to tell him what the car is doing. I'm not that involved in telling him what shocks and springs to put on it. But you've got to understand what the car is doing. If I don't know what's going on underneath, then it's going to be harder to push the limits. To push the limits, you have to push the limits of what's on the car. So I'd say at this point that I know more about the cars and the changes we make on them than I used to.

Have there been changes in the way fans respond to you over the years?
When I first started out, I built a fan base of people who really followed me. They were younger and older but not much in the middle, and I think there were more females. The thing about Dale Earnhardt was he conquered and got brought down and then he conquered again. He had such a solid core of fans and he connected to the core of fans in NASCAR because of that. I found out something similar by going through all the struggles in 2000 and clawing our way back up to the top. My fan base went down and people thought 'Uh-oh' and thought we were done. I had a lot drop off. Then when they saw me come back they said. 'Uh-oh,' I made a mistake and they climbed back on the bandwagon. I think they'll be there for a lot longer and stay with us through the highs and lows. I've always said this is who I am, this is what I like to do, this is the music I like and I like going to the movies or this, this and this. And I like God and I don't mind talking about it. Whoever is my fan will have to respect and appreciate my beliefs. It won't always be the majority of votes.

Would you prefer less emphasis on fans and sponsors and more emphasis on just racing?
I like the marketing and the advertising and getting involved in that side of the business. I like seeing the results, working on a commercial or an ad and then seeing what kind of impact it has. People saying they

Jeff Gordon

Above: *Gordon won two Daytona 500s and two Brickyard 400s before age 30. He tied the record for most modern era wins (13) in 1998 and later set a new mark with six straight road course victories.*

Above: Gordon not only helped build NASCAR's popularity among younger fans and women. By 2001, his race purses totaled $45.7 million and he took home millions more in souvenir sales plus endorsements.

saw it and liked it. Who doesn't like seeing themselves on television? But it's not like it controls me and eats me up. I don't want to be an actor. I like being a race car driver, but it's still fun to dabble in that. We can't do this sport without the fans, the sponsors and television. It all goes hand-in-hand. It's a part of it that I've got to just accept. There are days I wish it was a little more organized. You see people tripping and falling and doing insane things. I tell people all the time that race day at the track is the worst place to try to get an autograph. I tell people there are much better places to get a photo and an autograph without getting bloody.

Do you think that you have brought more of a corporate image to the sport?

We all came up at different times. When I came into racing, sponsorships were very important. My step-dad, John Bickford, got me into racing and he made me recognize that early on and that is was important being in front of people and calling on sponsors to get their money! I'd been on television on kid shows when I was younger with them doing various stories on me. I wasn't comfortable with it at first, but I grew to like it and understand that it was an important part of racing. When I first came into the Winston Cup maybe I was a little more polished. I think people recognized that here was a guy who was speaking in sentences with nouns, verbs and adjectives.

You certainly heard your share of boos due to your different approach.

At first when I started winning races and people started booing, I said 'what's up with that?' A lot of it started in '95 when we were racing Dale Earnhardt. We were wearing him out and were having a pretty good season. I realized a lot of boos were coming from Earnhardt fans. I realized that fans voice their opinions though jeers and cheers. Fans are out there fighting for me or their drivers. The real rivalries are in the grandstands.

Does the constant emphasis on images of drivers, such as good guys and bad guys, bother you?

I try to broaden my thoughts on the sport. We all start out as racers, racing Saturday nights on short tracks and just dreamed about being at this level. Then you get here and it's like 'Oh man!' Corporate politics and you have to be good to everybody. Then you say, 'Wait a minute! I don't want to do all these things.' As I grow older, I realize it's not only racing, it's entertainment. That's a part that you have to accept when you get in here. The sponsors are trying to gain customers and the networks are trying to gain viewers. NASCAR needs a good race, personalities, sponsors and fans in the stands. It's all about entertainment. When you start to understand this, you can go though all the things that you have to do in order to get into the race car and do what you do best. If you don't understand that, it will eat you alive. You'll stay up at night and worry about what some guy said about you in the media. It's got to be racing, but it also has to be entertainment.

To what extent do you consciously try to build an image for yourself?

I'm really doing what my heart and mind is leading me to do. I didn't plan the image. OK, I want to be this, this and this. I didn't do that. I'm a nice guy, I've always been clean cut and my parents taught me not to swear and to respect people. To me it's my personality, not an image. As a race car driver, I've always said I'll do what it takes to win. If on a given day it takes patience, I'll be patient. If it takes aggressiveness, I'll be aggressive. As a race car driver I don't want people to predict what I'm going to do. I want people to doubt what I might do at any given time other than give everything I've got in order to win. If a guy hits me and thinks I'm not going to hit him back, he's mistaken. I'm not some kid that was handed things on a golden platter. I've worked for my respect.

There have been moments of high anger from you on and off the track.

I don't think fans want to see me as Mr. Nice Guy all the time. These young guys are pushing it. They push the older guys. I'm in the middle, not older, but they are pushing.

You got started much younger than most of the drivers you've competed against in the Winston Cup. Does that mean you might retire at a younger age?

I've always said that as long as I have the desire, the health and the type of race team I've got at Hendrick Motorsports, I'm going to be out there driving the wheels off it as long as I can. I don't put an age limit or time limit on that. I don't know when that day will come. But it isn't going to happen any time soon and I'm happy to know that.

139

Jeff Gordon

Days of Gold

NASCAR and its participants struck it rich in the 1990s. The same man who brought stock car racing out of the backwoods and into prime time led the way, even in retirement. By the time Richard Petty hung up his helmet, his "Fan Appreciation Tour" had created a major new market for souvenir sales, which other drivers and the sanctioning body began to exploit.

On the same day "The King" said farewell after the 1992 season, another change took place with less fanfare. Dick Beaty retired as the Winston Cup Director. He had implemented NASCAR's change in policy from the star system to an even brighter approach—giving all entrants similar treatment when it came to rules enforcement. The ultimate result was an underdog owner/driver like Alan Kulwicki could win the championship, which he did on Beaty's final day.

Bill France Jr.'s emphasis on more winners and better competition had generated growth in fan interest, TV and corporate sponsorship. So the sport was ready for the modern marketplace, which by the 1990s included a multitude of cable channels hungry for hot properties with loyal viewing audiences.

Prosperity and the open door policy eventually led to the arrival of a young man from Indiana. Jeff Gordon put the final touch on stock car racing's battle with Indy-type racing for supremacy, becoming the biggest young racing star America had ever seen. Like Darrell Waltrip and Dale Earnhardt, he brought impassioned cheers and boos, but also created interest far beyond the usual boundaries.

Coupled with Earnhardt's intimidating success, NASCAR rode a wave of popularity. The sanctioning body then played an ace by signing a new TV contract for 2001. The billion-dollar network deal brought in a rising tide of cash confirming that stock car racing had joined football, baseball, basketball and hockey as a bona fide major league sport.

Above: *After his car caught fire in a multi-car crash in the final race of his career in Atlanta, Richard Petty joked, "I went out in a blaze, but I forgot the glory part." Petty returned for one final lap at the end of one of the races many people also consider the greatest in NASCAR history. Bill Elliott finished first, but lost the championship by ten points to Alan Kulwicki, who finished second that day. Kulwicki led the most laps, which gave him the necessary margin over Elliott for the title. Davey Allison entered the day in first place in his Robert Yates Racing Ford and needed only to finish in the Top Five to clinch the championship. But Allison was knocked out of the race by the spinning Chevy of Ernie Irvan with 72 laps to go while running sixth. A 21-year-old named Jeff Gordon started his first Winston Cup race that day, had an accident and finished 31st.*

Right: *Kulwicki drove his Ford "Underbird" to one of the unlikeliest championship seasons in NASCAR history. After the 22nd round at Dover, Del. and with seven races remaining, the Wisconsin driver trailed leader Bill Elliott and Junior Johnson's veteran team by 278 points. Plus, he had wrecked three cars during the Dover weekend. But during the stretch drive, Johnson and wife Flossie began divorce proceedings and a political power struggle broke out in the Ingles Hollow, N.C. shops of the team, technically owned by Flossie as a result of Johnson's bootlegging days. A nose-dive in the points by Elliott enabled Kulwicki, the only owner/driver winning races at the time, to catch him by season's end. In the beginning of a tragic span for NASCAR, Kulwicki was killed in the crash of a private plane owned by sponsor Hooters the following April while en route to a race in Bristol, Tenn.*

Days of Gold

Above: *When Roger Penske returned to NASCAR, he hired Rusty Wallace as a partner along with Don Miller, then they took Victory Lane by storm. From 1990–96, Wallace won 28 races and led in victories in 1993 (10) and 1994 (8).*

Right: *Davey Allison's replacement, Ernie Irvan contended Earnhardt for the championship in 1994. But a near-fatal practice crash at Michigan left him with eyesight problems. Irvan ran only 20 races, but still led the most miles in '94. He returned to Yates and won three races before switching to MB2 and then retiring in 1999.*

Oppostie page: *Davey Allison won the Daytona 500 in 1992 and managed to stay in the running for the championship despite a horrifying 11-flip crash at Pocono. He also won The Winston despite getting knocked unconscious when Kyle Petty hit his Ford at the finish. When he crashed his own helicopter in the infield at Talladega in July of 1993, Allison's streak of surviving bad crashes ended due to a fatal head injury. In a tragic spell for the Allison family, brother Clifford died in a Busch Series crash at Michigan the previous year.*

Days of Gold

Above: *During his comeback from a 1990 head injury, Neil Bonnett crashed fatally at Daytona in 1994. This photo shows his Chevy after a right rear shock mount broke, which led to the crash moments later.*

Below: *Officials at Winston worried about empty seats at the massive Indianapolis Motor Speedway prior to the first Brickyard 400 in 1994. But it was a sell-out long before Indiana favorite Jeff Gordon won it.*

Opposite page: *Dale Earnhardt won his seventh Winston Cup championship in style with a victory at Rockingham by half a car length over Rick Mast. After his win he dedicated the day to fallen friend Bonnett.*

Left: *Ray Evernham became the first crew chief to hire a full-time pit crew when he put together the Rainbow Warriors. Time and again, this crew made cat-quick pit stops for driver Jeff Gordon. In addition to mounting fresh tires and adding fuel, the stops often included chassis changes on the Hendrick Motorsports Chevy by use of spring rubbers, jackscrews for the chassis and track bar without any substantial loss of time.*

The ability to make changes quickly became a foundation in the success of Gordon. Once back on the track, the driver's willingness to drive deep into the corners with new set-ups underneath him was the crucial variable. More often than not, Evernham's ability to make the right calls and Gordon's driving talent made the system work.

Evernham would arrive at the tracks with several different spring and shock set-ups to experiment with during the initial practice; they would all go on the car no matter what the results. The information returned from such constant chassis changes throughout all the practices gave Evernham a comprehensive log that helped make his mid-race decisions so effective.

Gordon's role was to tell Evernham the characteristics of the car's handling. During races, the changes sometimes did not sit well with the driver, who voiced his uneasiness via radio and needed coaxing from his crew chief to "hang on." More often than any other team, including other entries from Hendrick Motorsports, they ended up hanging on to the trophy.

Above: Sterling Marlin didn't end his racing family's collective 443-race losing streak until he joined Morgan-McClure in 1994. Marlin then won two straight Daytona 500s. Father Clifton "Coo Coo" Marlin said it was justice done, charging that NASCAR brought him into the pits during the 1974 Daytona 500 for a non-existent lug nut problem so a star driver could win. After leading four times, "Coo Coo" finished fourth behind winner Richard Petty.

Right: Jeff Gordon and Ray Evernham figured out Daytona quickly. Gordon won the 20-lap Busch Clash exhibition his first try at age 22, beating Dale Earnhardt and Ernie Irvan with a surprise three-wide pass in Turn 2. Gordon put Earnhardt on his roof en route to his first Daytona 500 trophy in 1997 and won it again in 1999.

Days of Gold

152

Above: *Dale Earnhardt's Chevy was caught in a multi-car crash at Talladega in 1996 and collected two licks from other cars, including one in the roof. The driver limped away from the wreckage despite a broken collar bone and sternum, then insisted the ambulance driver stop on pit road so Earnhardt could tell his crew he was alright. Earnhardt did not miss a start and won the pole at Watkins Glen two weeks later. A neck injury was not discovered until much later and after disc surgery prior to the 1999 season, "The Intimidator" returned to form.*

Opposite page: *"The King" and wife Lynda returned to Victory Lane with Petty Enterprises for the first time in 13 seasons when Bobby Hamilton drove No. 43 to victory at Phoenix. Richard Petty moved to Mike Curb's team after the 1983 engine scandal, winning his final two races there. Kyle Petty operated Petty Enterprises from Level Cross, N.C. for one year. Richard returned in 1986 until retirement in 1992. Rick Wilson, Wally Dallenbach Jr. and John Andretti preceded Hamilton in the wheelhouse. Dale Inman (not shown) won seven championships with his cousin Richard Petty, one with Terry Labonte and was the spotter for Hamilton.*

Days of Gold

Above: High-grooving Dale
Earnhardt won a record nine races
at the Atlanta Motor Speedway,
starting with his first
superspeedway win for Rod
Osterlund's team and crew chief
Jake Elder in 1980. NASCAR's only
true oval, Atlanta was a 1.5-mile
model of the longer Indianapolis
Motor Speedway. The sweeping
turns, multiple grooves and high
speeds made it possible for a driver
with the right amount of touch and
guts to coax more speed from his
car. Owner Bruton Smith re-built the
track into his "quad-oval" design to
increase grandstand seating in the
fall of 1997.

Opposite page below: *Rick Hendrick was the first to build a three-car team in the modern era. Shown here talking with Ken Schrader, who won two races with crew chief Harry Hyde at Hendrick Motorsports, the car dealer won three races in his first season, 1984, with Geoff Bodine. By 2001, Hendrick had added 100 more victories and earned $93.4 million in prize money.*

Above: *En route to Victory Lane after finally winning the Daytona 500 in 1998, Dale Earnhardt received high fives from many of the crew members of rival teams on pit road. He spun two huge doughnuts through the track logo in the grass before celebrating on the roof of his car. When Earnhardt arrived in the press box, he pulled a stuffed toy monkey from his driving suit and hurled it into the air. "I've got that (expletive deleted) monkey off my back!" he shouted.*

It was quite a different ending from the year before, when another chapter had been added to the litany of his bad luck in 19 previous attempts. The front tire changer for Richard Childress Racing had been fired the morning of the race for missing his wake-up call and Earnhardt was tardy out of the pits for much of the race. A final two-tire stop by crew chief Larry McReynolds to get track position backfired when Jeff Gordon passed Earnhardt in Turn 2. The "Intimidator" didn't back off and ended up in the Turn 2 wall and then on his roof in a long skid down the back straight. The car eventually righted itself and Earnhardt clambered out. Once he realized all four wheels were still on it, he jumped back in and finished the race.

Opposite page top: *When Dale Jarrett switched crew chiefs in 1996, dropping Larry McReynolds in favor of Todd Parrott, he began a hot streak for Robert Yates Racing. The second-generation driver won 18 races in four seasons, culminating with the 1999 Winston Cup.*

Opposite page bottom: *Mark Martin finished second in the championship three times in the 1990s. In 1998, he won seven races, the same year Jeff Gordon had his 13-win season. But Martin did beat everybody to the first Winston Cup trophy in Las Vegas.*

Right: *Just as the France family's International Speedway Corporation followed Bruton Smith's example of going public with his tracks, Daytona followed the Charlotte facility owned by Smith in putting up lights for night racing on its superspeedway.*

Below: *Jeff Gordon does it again. The winner of the first night race in Daytona, Gordon was late to Victory Lane. The race originally was scheduled for July, but had to be run in October due to wildfires that swept Florida in the summer of 1998.*

157

Days of Gold

Above left: *The whiz kids took Daytona's trophy home a second time in 1999, but by the following year would go their separate ways after 216 races, 47 victories and three championships. Gordon turned down Evernham's offer to join his new Dodge team and instead decided to become a part owner at Hendrick Motorsports.*

Above right: *Joe Gibbs will be the only man to ever win the National Football League's championship three times and the Winston Cup as well. Gibbs said his interest in fast cars started when he listened to the police radio in his North Carolina home town while his father, the sheriff, chased bootleggers. After winning the Daytona 500 with Dale Jarrett, Gibbs' driver Bobby Labonte won the title in 2000.*

Opposite page: *Gibbs signed Tony Stewart and got the former Indy Racing League champion to commit to NASCAR's Winston Cup. Stewart's record was initially better than fellow Hoosier Jeff Gordon and he led the series in victories in his sophomore season with six. In 1999, rookie Stewart became the first driver to move from the back of the pack to the front in the 600-mile race at Charlotte after finishing ninth in the Indy 500 earlier in the day. Stewart, who finished a dehydrated fourth, started in the back due to missing NASCAR's pre-race drivers' meeting.*

Above: *Ray Evernham may have lost Jeff Gordon, but he gained his own team and a multi-million dollar budget when Dodge hired him to direct the DaimlerChrysler brand's return to NASCAR in 2000.*

Left: *In 1999, Dale Jarrett became the first driver to follow his father to NASCAR's premier championship. Ned and Dale introduced South Florida to the year-end celebration after the first appearance by the Winston Cup at the Homestead-Miami track built by Ralph Sanchez. Where Ned won a paltry sum and became a track promoter and announcer after winning his second title in 1965, son Dale took home $6.6 million during his banner year.*

Above and below: Dale Earnhardt might have won the Daytona 500 earlier without the presence of Dale Jarrett. "The Intimidator" got passed by Jarrett's Chevy on the last lap in 1993. Jarrett beat pole winner and runner-up Earnhardt's Chevy again in 1996 in the Robert Yates Racing Ford. Jarrett took his third Daytona trophy home in 1999, passing Mark Martin in the late stages.

Oposite page top: In 2000, Bobby Labonte won one of the most bizarre Southern 500s at a Darlington track known for unusual events. He pitted during a yellow for rainfall, then returned to the track in first place. After one lap, the race was halted and never re-started. It was the only lap Labonte led all day.

Oposite page below: Labonte (right) and Joe Gibbs Racing crew members kiss the yard of bricks at Indy after winning the Brickyard 400. The win paid $831,225 and helped launch the Texan to the $3 million Winston Cup, joining two-time champion brother Terry Labonte.

Above: Mike Helton became the first president of NASCAR other than a France family member when he was given the job in November of 2000 by Chairman of the Board Bill France Jr., who had been undergoing treatment for cancer. At that time, a five-person governing board was established for NASCAR, including France Jr.'s younger brother Jim, and France Jr.'s two children, Lesa France Kennedy and Brian France. As the NASCAR president, Helton also became a member of the new board. Previously, Bill and Jim France "met in the hall" at NASCAR headquarters to make many of NASCAR's decisions, said the older brother.

Right: Helton, who had worked as NASCAR's vice president before his promotion, found the going tough in his first year. The first points race he presided over in 2001 was the last for the No. 3 Chevy of Dale Earnhardt, killed by a Turn 4 crash on the last lap of the Daytona 500. The previous season, three other drivers—the Winston Cup's Kenny Irwin, Craftsman Truck Series driver Tony Roper and Busch Series competitor Adam Petty—had also died of head injuries. Helton directed NASCAR's post-accident investigation following the Earnhardt crash and launched the sport's most comprehensive safety and technology development campaign under the glare of an irate and impatient media.

Below: The vigil begins as fires burn late in the infield at Daytona in Turn 4, where the flag stood at half-mast. It was the beginning of an unprecedented outpouring of grief for a fallen NASCAR hero. (See overleaf.)

Above: Had Earnhardt's car not been pivoted by the Pontiac of Ken Schrader just before both hit the wall, the outcome might have been different. As it was, the head-on angle meant the g-loads were too much for Earnhardt.

Opposite page: Hail the new dominator. Jeff Gordon took over as the sport's biggest star by the end of 2001, winning his fourth Winston Cup. His record $10.9 million season gave him the top spot in career earnings.

Rusty Cook
Toni Evans
Matt Evans
Austin
Garrison #3
God Bless
We Always Loved
The McCormick
We Will Miss You
Erich & Denise Bradley
Buffalo NY

Records

NASCAR WINSTON CUP CHAMPIONS

Year	Car No.	Champion Driver	Champion Owner	Make Car	Race Wins
1949a	22	Red Byron	Raymond Parks	Oldsmobile	2
1950b	60	Bill Rexford	Julian Buesink	Oldsmobile	1
1951	92	Herb Thomas	Herb Thomas	Hudson	7
1952	91	Tim Flock	Ted Chester	Hudson	8
1953	92	Herb Thomas	Herb Thomas	Hudson	11
1954	92	-	Herb Thomas*	Hudson	12
	42	Lee Petty	-	Chrysler	7
1955	300	Tim Flock	Carl Kiekhaefer	Chrysler	18
1956	300B	Buck Baker	Carl Kiekhaefer	Chrysler	14
1957	87	Buck Baker	Buck Baker	Chevrolet	10
1958	42	Lee Petty	Petty Entrp.	Oldsmobile	7
1959	42	Lee Petty	Petty Entrp.	Plymouth	10
1960	4	Rex White	White-Clements	Chevrolet	6
1961	11	Ned Jarrett	W.G. Holloway, Jr	Chevrolet	1
1962	8	Joe Weatherly	Bud Moore	Pontiac	9
1963	21	-	Wood Brothers*	Ford	3
	8	Joe Weatherly*	-	Mercury	3
1964	43	Richard Petty	Petty Entrp.	Plymouth	9
1965	11	Ned Jarrett	Bondy Long	Ford	13
1966	6	David Pearson	Cotton Owens	Dodge	14
1967	43	Richard Petty	Petty Entrp.	Plymouth	27
1968	17	David Pearson	Holman-Moody	Ford	16

1969	17	David Pearson	Holman-Moody	Ford	11
1970	71	Bobby Isaac	Nord Krauskopf	Dodge	11
1971	43	Richard Petty	Petty Entrp.	Plymouth	21
1972c	43	Richard Petty	Petty Entrp.	Plymouth	8
1973	72	Benny Parsons	L.G. DeWitt	Chevrolet	1
1974	43	Richard Petty	Petty Entrp.	Dodge	10
1975	43	Richard Petty	Petty Entrp.	Dodge	13
1976	11	Cale Yarborough	Junior Johnson	Chevrolet	9
1977	11	Cale Yarborough	Junior Johnson	Chevrolet	9
1978	11	Cale Yarborough	Junior Johnson	Oldsmobile	10
1979	43	Richard Petty	Petty Entrp.	Chevrolet	5
1980	2	Dale Earnhardt	Rod Osterlund	Chevrolet	5
1981	11	Darrell Waltrip	Junior Johnson	Buick	12
1982	11	Darrell Waltrip	Junior Johnson	Buick	12
1983	22	Bobby Allison	Bill Gardner	Buick	6
1984	44	Terry Labonte	Billy Hagan	Chevrolet	2
1985	11	Darrell Waltrip	Junior Johnson	Chevrolet	3
1986	3	Dale Earnhardt	Richard Childress	Chevrolet	5
1987	3	Dale Earnhardt	Richard Childress	Chevrolet	11
1988	9	Bill Elliott	Harry Melling	Ford	6
1989	27	Rusty Wallace	Raymond Beadle	Pontiac	6
1990	3	Dale Earnhardt	Richard Childress	Chevrolet	9
1991	3	Dale Earnhardt	Richard Childress	Chevrolet	4
1992	7	Alan Kulwicki	Alan Kulwicki	Ford	2
1993	3	Dale Earnhardt	Richard Childress	Chevrolet	6
1994	3	Dale Earnhardt	Richard Childress	Chevrolet	4
1995	24	Jeff Gordon	Rick Hendrick	Chevrolet	7
1996	5	Terry Labonte	Rick Hendrick	Chevrolet	2
1997	24	Jeff Gordon	Rick Hendrick	Chevrolet	10
1998	24	Jeff Gordon	Rick Hendrick	Chevrolet	13
1999	88	Dale Jarrett	Robert Yates	Ford	4
2000	18	Bobby Labonte	Joe Gibbs Racing	Pontiac	4
2001	24	Jeff Gordon	Rick Hendrick	Chevrolet	6

*Won Driver or Owner Championship; a= known as Strictly Stock Division; b= renamed Grand National Division; c= renamed Winston Cup Series.

ALL-TIME WINSTON CUP RACE WINNERS

Rank	Driver	Wins	Rank	Driver	Wins
1	Richard Petty*	200	22	Jim Paschal*	25
2	David Pearson*	105	23	Joe Weatherly#	22
3	Darrell Waltrip	84	24	Ricky Rudd	22
	Bobby Allison*	84	25	Jack Smith#	21
5	Cale Yarborough*	83		Terry Labonte	21
6	Dale Earnhardt#	76		Benny Parsons*	21
7	Jeff Gordon	58	28	Speedy Thompson#	20
8	Lee Petty*	54	29	Buddy Baker*	19
	Rusty Wallace	54		Fonty Flock#	19
10	Junior Johnson*	50		Davey Allison#	19
	Ned Jarrett*	50	32	Harry Gant*	18
12	Herb Thomas#	48		Neil Bonnett#	18
13	Buck Baker*	46		Geoff Bodine	18
14	Bill Elliott	41	35	Marvin Panch*	17
15	Tim Flock#	40		Curtis Turner#	17
16	Bobby Isaac#	37		Jeff Burton	17
17	Fireball Roberts#	34	38	Ernie Irvan	15
18	Mark Martin	29	39	Dick Hutcherson*	14
19	Dale Jarrett	28		LeeRoy Yarbrough#	14
20	Fred Lorenzen*	26			
	Rex White*	26			

*Retired #Deceased In the 1,950 races during the period there have been 162 drivers who have won at least one event.

Records

ALL-TIME WINSTON CUP POLE WINNERS

Rank	Driver	Poles
1	Richard Petty*	126
2	David Pearson*	113
3	Cale Yarborough*	70
4	Darrell Waltrip	59
5	Bobby Allison*	57
6	Bobby Isaac#	51
	Bill Elliott	51
8	Junior Johnson*	47
9	Buck Baker*	44
10	Mark Martin	41
11	Buddy Baker*	40
	Jeff Gordon	40
13	Herb Thomas#	39
	Tim Flock#	39
15	Geoff Bodine	37
16	Fireball Roberts#	35
	Ned Jarrett*	35
	Rex White*	35
19	Fonty Flock#	34
20	Fred Lorenzen*	33
21	Ricky Rudd	27
22	Terry Labonte	26
23	Jack Smith#	24
	Alan Kulwicki#	24
25	Ken Schrader	23
26	Dale Earnhardt#	22
	Dick Hutcherson*	22

*Retired #Deceased
In the 1,944 races where time trials were held (or records kept), there have been 189 drivers who have won pole positions.

Records

WINS BY CAR MAKE (1949-2001)

Ford	517	Buick	65
Chevrolet	497	Chrysler	59
Plymouth	190	Thunderbird*	6
Dodge	168	AMC Matador	5
Pontiac	148	Lincoln	4
Oldsmobile	116	Studebaker	3
Mercury	96	Nash	1
Hudson	79	Jaguar	1

*Thunderbird listed as separate make in 1959. Now included under Ford. Three other races won by Grand American Division cars (i.e. Chevrolet Camaro, Ford Mustang) in combined events not shown in above totals for 1,950 races.

TOP 20 MONEY WINNERS IN WINSTON CUP RACING (1949-Dec. 2001)

Rank	Driver	Races	Wins	Money Won
1	Jeff Gordon	293	58	$45,566,580
2	Dale Earnhardt	676	76	41,742,384
3	Dale Jarrett	459	28	33,274,832
4	Rusty Wallace	526	54	24,869,067
5	Mark Martin	494	32	29,165,322
6	Bill Elliott	659	41	27,506,174
7	Terry Labonte	709	21	26,536,692
8	Bobby Labonte	294	17	25,953,024
9	Ricky Rudd	731	22	24,530,233
10	Jeff Burton	259	17	22,958,499
11	Sterling Marlin	539	8	19,899,539
12	Darrell Waltrip*	809	84	19,416,618
13	Ken Schrader	528	4	18,124,281
14	Geoff Bodine	552	18	14,831,269
15	Michael Waltrip	498	1	14,829,876
16	Kyle Petty	609	8	13,331,568
17	Ward Burton	250	3	13,023,311
18	Bobby Hamilton	337	4	12,990,059
19	Brett Bodine	442	1	11,425,453
20	Ernie Irvan*	292	15	10,552,042

Records

The publishers would like to thank the following sources for their kind permission to reproduce the pictures in this book:

Getty Images: 135, 137/ Richard Dole 168-9, Jon Ferrey 1, 138, 159, Darrell Ingham 164-5, Robert Laberge 163b, 166t, Donald Miralle 132-3, 140, Jamie Squire 4, 158tl, 162tl, 166b, 167.

Daytona Racing Archive: 47b, 48t, 48bl, 48br, 50b, 52-3, 54b, 55, 56, 57tl, 57br, 58, 59b, 60b, 60tl, 61t, 64t, 66-7, 68-9, 79, 80, 81, 82, 87, 88-9, 90b, 92-3, 94t, 95b, 96t, 98b, 98tl, 99b, 99t, 100-1, 105, 107, 110, 113t, 114t, 114b, 115tl, 118, 119t, 119br, 120, 121t, 121, 124br, 125b, 128bl, 129b, 131, 142, 147, 148-9, 150tl, 150-1, 152, 153, 154t, 154br, 155, 156t, 156b, 157tr, 157b, 158tr, 160-1, 161tr, 162b, 163t, 164tl.

Courtesy of Mike Jensen: 7

Courtesy of Raymond Parks: 8, 25

Dozier Mobley Photography: 2-3, 3, 10-1, 13, 14, 15, 16, 17, 18, 20bl, 20t, 21b, 21tr, 22bl, 22t, 23, 24, 26t, 26bl, 27, 28t, 28br, 29t, 29b, 30-1, 32bl, 32t, 33, 34, 35tr, 35b, 36-7, 39, 40, 43, 44, 46, 47b, 47t, 49, 50tl, 51, 54t, 59t, 61b, 62-3, 64b, 65, 71, 73, 74, 75, 76, 78t, 78b, 83t, 83br, 84-5, 86, 89tr, 89br, 90t, 91t, 91b, 94b, 95t, 96b, 97, 103, 104, 108, 111b, 111t, 112, 113br, 115tr, 115b, 116-7, 122t, 122b, 123, 124t, 125tr, 126t, 126b, 127, 128t, 128br, 129t, 130, 144, 145, 145b, 146t, 146b.

Every effort has been made to acknowledge correctly and contact the source and/or copyright holder of each picture, and Carlton Books Limited apologises for any unintentional errors or omissions which will be corrected in future editions of this book.

The publishers wish to express their sincere gratitude to Dozier Mobley for the time and assistance he has contributed to this project.